FRUGAL FAMILIES

Making the Most of Your Hard Earned Money

Jonni McCoy

FRUGAL FAMILIES
Making the Most of
Your Hard Earned Money

ISBN 1-888306-50-5

Cover and book design
by Mark E. & Wendy E. Dinsmore
Arkworks@aol.com

Cover Illustration by Brian E. Stuck

For information contact

Full Quart Press an imprint of Holly Hall Publications, Inc.
P.O. Box 254
Elkton, MD 21922-0254

Note from the publisher and the author

This book is based upon personal experience, interviews, and research by the author. Although much effort was made to ensure that all information in the book is safe and accurate, this book is sold with the understanding that the author and publisher assume no responsibility for oversights, discrepancies, or inaccuracies. This book is not intended to replace medical, financial, legal, or other professional advice. Readers are reminded to use their own good judgment before applying any ideas found within this book.

Printed in the United States of America.

DEDICATION

I dedicate this book to my dear family.
To my husband, Beau,
for his constant belief in me
and his endless research, ideas, and support
that made this book what it is.
And to my children,
Jeremy and Jessica,
for their patience and interest.

ACKNOWLEDGMENTS

I would like to acknowledge the valuable help given to me by my friends, Craig and Kat Osten, and by Jan Dennis. And to my friend and editor, Heather Armstrong, for taking care of all of us.

TABLE OF CONTENTS

Frugality Runamuck: Introduction

1. Getting Home 11
2. Kids 21
   - Teaching Kids Financial Responsibility 21
   - Lunch Boxes 25
   - Clothes 28
   - Pets 30
   - Kids Activities 39
3. Gardening 45
4. Fun In The Sun/Vacations 59
5. Money, Money 81
6. Insurance 99
   - Homeowners Insurance 99
   - Car Insurance 105
   - Life Insurance 108
   - Medical Insurance 115
   - Disability Insurance 125
   - Vision 126
   - Doctor Bills 127
   - Hospital Bills 129
   - Medications 132
   - Dental Expenses 135
7. Help Around the House/Electronics & Appliances 139
8. Furnishing Your Home 147
9. Car Buying 155
10. Making Your Car Last/Car Maintenance 165
11. Computers for the Technologically Challenged 173
12. I Can't Take It Any More!/Consumer Rights 197

Resources 207
Index 232

INTRODUCTION

Frugality Runamuck

It is a great mistake to suppose that economy consists in buying the poorest articles and in making the table unattractive.

–Anonymous, Buckeye Cookery, 1881

Frugality has received a bad reputation through the years. This reputation keeps many people in financial bondage. Some of these people are women who would like to be at home with their family, but fear what frugality means. Some are families who are in debt and unable to reduce that burden because they don't know a better way of managing their money.

It's understandable how people have misunderstood frugality. We hear other frugal authors suggesting uses for dryer lint (I think it belongs in the garbage can) or reusing plastic wrap. Some frugal folks wear stained and torn clothing in the name of frugality. These are examples of frugality runamuck.

True frugality should have something to show for itself. If you are going to be frugal, make it count for something. I bake from scratch because it saves on my grocery bill, not because I like that homey feeling. I shop resale clothing stores to save half on clothing, not to be cheap. Some die-hard frugals wash out baggies. I don't since they cost me about 1¢. Using cloth napkins instead of paper saves about $4 per month. If you choose to do these things for conservation measures, that's fine. But these are not the core of frugality.

Frugality should be a means to an end: a way to make your home what you desire. I don't see it as endless energy spent on minor savings. I am frugal so I can be at home with my children. I want to spend as much time with them as possible, so my frugality must be carefully chosen. I don't want my time filled with saving soap slivers and aluminum foil. To decide if a frugal activity is worth my time, I figure out what the savings will be for my time spent on that activity.

We must choose how we fill our days. Nobody can do it all. Find the activities that save the most money and drop the rest. Your family and friends are more important. Play with your kids. Plant a garden. Read a book.

CHAPTER ONE

Getting Home

No job can compete with the responsibility of shaping and molding a new human being.

–Dr. James Dobson

During the past 20 years, two income families have risen by 60%; and coincidentally, divorce has risen by 34%.[1] This is happening despite survey statistics which show that 80% of parents believe that one parent should be at home with the children, and 75% of working women claim that they place family over work.[2] What makes these families live contrary to their beliefs? Money.

We lived with this same dichotomy for several years. As a senior buyer at Apple Computer, I had a great career that I didn't want to give up. I liked the extra income, and I enjoyed the personal challenge that the job brought me. But I also felt the tug of wanting to do a better job as a mom and wife at home. Adding to my struggle was the fatigue and stress that comes with trying to be good in both worlds. Finally, after 3 1/2 years, I decided to take the plunge and quit. Since I made 50% of the income, this was going to be tough. Living in the third most expensive area in the nation (San Francisco Bay Area), didn't help either.

We originally didn't think it could be done, and planned to move into the suburbs. But I wanted to stay where we were. We were able to keep our home and our cars, while adding another child to the family.

I learned to cut back in ways I never knew one could. I cut groceries down to $40 per week for four people, and kept our clothing expenses down to $350 for the year. I cut every area of our budget to make my goal of staying home. And it worked.

THE PROBLEM

Many women want to stay home, but are afraid of what being frugal will do to them or their family. They have visions of making disgusting choices, or fearing severe deprivation. I feared these things, too. Living frugally didn't come naturally for me. I spent six years overseas with my parents, where we lived an upper class lifestyle. We had five servants and traveled the world to exotic locations. Later, my parents graciously paid for my four years at a university. I was accustomed to good things. But I took the plunge anyway because of my desire to be an at-home mom. And I am living proof that living frugally doesn't mean giving up your sense of class.

A national survey[3] was conducted among several national mothers' organizations, asking for the main reasons that parents wanted to be at home. Here are the top 8 reasons given:

- *we felt it was the best way to raise our child*
- *we didn't want to miss our child's childhood*
- *we wanted to raise our child with our values*
- *my emotional attachment was too strong to leave the child*
- *my work load was too heavy*
- *my work schedule was too inflexible*
- *we couldn't find adequate childcare*
- *we couldn't afford adequate childcare*

Some experts fear that the fatigue, stress and alienation that comes with both parents working is causing a social crisis in America. They feel that the isolation people are experiencing is causing a breakdown in communities and families. I have a friend who is a student advisor at a university. She has seen a drastic difference in the students who have enrolled during the past five years, as compared to those fifteen years ago. In her opinion, they are immature and lack most life skills. She credits the lack of an at-home parent as a main cause.

Many family counselors have been quoted as saying that children need more than the best that a caregiver can provide. According to Dr. Jay Belsky, a Penn State psychologist who conducted extensive research on the effects of childcare, babies who don't form an attachment with one main provider will have less self-control and will be less cooperative as they mature.

Behavioral problems tend to plague these children as they get older. [4] Other researchers have found that children who grow up in daycare may do better academically, but tend to be more hyperactive, less curious, less responsive to adults, have poor relationships, and are less altruistic. And, unfortunately, most working mothers have children under the age of six. These children need their mom, especially during those early years.

Many psychologists believe that children need the stability of an available parent, and the community that comes from their home and the neighborhood.[5] These same experts state that good families are a conscious choice and effort, and don't just happen.

There are parents who feel they are bad at parenting, and that their children are better off in someone else's care. Don't believe that lie! No one is better suited for a child's care than his parents. Parents hold the key to their child's heart.

Whether or not the conclusions made by these experts are true for your family, only you can decide. Some parents have effectively balanced their working and at-home lives. Some may yearn for a more peaceful lifestyle, and more time with their children. If the latter is your situation, there may be a way for you to come home.

COST OF WORKING

Surprisingly, many may find that having one person at home might actually cost them less, and be less stressful. This may sound strange, but I found it to be true. When I chose to stay at home with my children, we assumed we would have to move to a less expensive suburb to compensate for the 50% loss of income. But when I couldn't go through with the move, we were in a pickle. Same house. Same lifestyle. Half the money. Even though I wanted to be at home full time, out of desperation I looked at working part-time. It was then that I realized how much working had cost.

Financial experts have calculated the cost of working at anywhere from $9 to $25 per hour. I was stunned when I learned this! That meant that if I took a job paying $10 per hour, I would only see $1 for every hour that I worked.

One man earned $28 per hour, but his earning power (wage less cost of working) was only $2.65 per hour. When I buy something now, I think of how many hours of work it really cost us. It makes things seem less desirable.

Here are the expenses figured into these experts' calculations:

child care
taxes (local, federal, state)
commuting fees (tolls, parking, etc.)
gasoline and mileage
car insurance (extra car, nicer car for the job, etc.)
clothes (new clothes, cleaners, accessories, etc.)
gifts for co-workers
fast-food lunches and breakfasts
convenience foods at home
extra eating out
occasional housekeeping help
hair care

Every person has a different cost of working. Some people have several children in daycare, while others have no children. Some commute many miles to work, others ride a bike. Some can wear casual clothes to work while others are required to dress in suits. Some pay more taxes than others. With this list, you can factor your own cost of working.

We found we could save plenty with me at home. Many expenses disappeared that we had not planned on. First, our taxes went down into a lower bracket without my salary. Second, our food costs went down. We ate out less (eating out costs six times more than making it at home) and cut our grocery bill by 60% with shopping and cooking changes. Third, I had time to shop for sale prices on all items from food to clothing to furniture. Fourth, we needed less work-related items (salon haircuts, new clothes, dry cleaners, and office gifts). And finally, we needed less "stress busters" in order to do all that a family requires.

MAKING THE CHOICE

Some parents truly are unable to cut their income any further, and require both parents to work. I have met many who are "stuck" there, and my heart goes out to them as they do their best to juggle their lifestyle. Many ache for their children as they go off to work, and rejoice when they reunite in the evening. These folks are doing what they can.

Other families have been able to pay the cost of following their convictions. There are three women whose stories of personal cost are worth knowing about. These ladies made major sacrifices in order to stay at home. One example is Helen Jackson, a NASA employee, who was slated to be the first black woman astronaut. She had earned scholarships to MIT and John Hopkins, and was in line for space travel. But she watched her children flounder. They did poorly in school and had social problems. They needed the stability of a parent at home. Helen gave up her career to be there for them. And they responded. She never has looked back in regret. The career she chose of molding those kids was more important to her.

Another woman I know wanted very much to be at home full-time. She had been a working parent for four years, and she and her husband had accumulated $42,000 in debt. She took the plunge for the sake of her child, and is living frugally in order to do so. She is not incurring any further debt, and is slowly paying down the existing debt. Most families would have chosen two incomes in order to pay down the debt.

Last, but not least, is a friend who has four children. Her husband works at a low wage and receives no benefits. They also pay child support for his son from a previous marriage. They live meagerly, but happily. They have their stresses over finances, but they know it's better for her to be at home right now. So sacrifices are made—for now. They know it gets better with time.

Once you are willing to make some changes, the plunge doesn't seem so overwhelming. The challenge is being willing. And amazingly, 69% of all parents say they want a simpler life.[6]

So, what is keeping people at work when they want to be at home? The biggest concern is money. Many fear the loss of one job, so the other parent works, "just in case." Many can't stand the idea of being at home all day with little kids. Others reasons are more complicated. Here are a sampling of the main reasons parents give for remaining at work:

Society

There is an unfortunate lack of identity for the at-home mom. Many say, "That's all you do?" The at-home mom has no title, promotions, raises or pats on the back. Of the moms surveyed, 28% said the hardest part of quitting was the loss of professional status.[7] Not surprisingly, more affluent moms go back to work as often as low-income moms. It's not just for the money. If a lack of identity is an issue, volunteer work can give that immediate sense of approval.

Raising a child should be seen as a ministry, not as something that gets in the way of our careers or other interests. Down the road, your pleasure in seeing a finished product in your adult child will be your triumph. Even though the moms that were surveyed said that they had a hard time with the loss of job status, 35% said they felt more at peace with themselves after quitting.[8]

Spousal Support

A spouse that is at home is often taken for granted by the working spouse. Of the spouses surveyed, most were supportive of the other spouse's decision to leave work.[9] That leaves 24% that were unhappy, unconcerned or outright unsupportive. The working spouse is clueless as to the day to day stress of an at-home parent. Your identity in their mind will change. If this is the case, the at-home mom may need reinforcement from other moms or outside involvements.

Education

Many women feel they betray their training and education if they quit. They feel they need to use the years and the price of their education. Many women have lost their marriages due to the pursuit of utilizing their education. Remember that your "new" career is to prepare tomorrow's leader, and mold a person into adulthood.

Loneliness

The loss of a peer group at work and the monotony of being at home scares many people. Getting involved in a community college, kids play groups, clubs, churches, or volunteer groups provides that new support group.

Examples of National At-Home Mother Support Groups

La Leche League – Nursing moms support group
1400 N. Meacham Rd.
Schaumburg, IL 60173-4048
(847) 519-7730
http://lalecheleague.org/

FEMALE (Formerly Employed Mothers at Loose Ends)
Support group for mothers who left a career
P.O. Box 31
Elmhurst, IL 60126
(708) 941-3553
http://FEMALEhome.org/home.htm

Hearts at Home
900 West College
Normal, IL 61761
(309) 888-MOMS
http://www.hearts-at-home.org/

The National MOMS Club
Supports at-home mothers
2531 Rye Canyon Rd
Valencia, CA 91355
e-mail: momsclub@aol.com

MOPS International (Mothers Of Preschools)
Christian support group for mothers of preschoolers
1311 South Clarkson
Denver, CO 80210
(303) 733-5353
http://www.mops.org

Mothers At Home, Inc.
Offers a national newsletter called "Welcome Home"
8310-A Old Courthouse Road
Vienna, VA 22182
(800) 783-4666
http://www.mah.org/

Just In Case

The fear of one spouse losing a job, or the instability of one of the spouse's income will keep many spouses working. Other women fear that, if they ever divorce, they would need to be working in order to survive. These can be real fears. Only they can decide if they should listen to the fears, or step out in faith.

Job Mobility

Many fear they will never be able to return to their current level in their career. Don't let fear of the future interfere with what you believe is right for today. Besides, you may change. When you return to work, you may have different interests. And the skills you acquire at home or doing volunteer work may be useful in a future career.

Cost of Living

The cost of living increases shouldn't be an obstacle either. The cost of living is about the same as it was ninety years ago[10] (factoring in adjustments for inflation). We just want more than our elders did. We want it bigger, faster and more convenient. Perhaps this statistic helps explain our trend: the average American spends six hours per week shopping, but only forty minutes per week playing with their kids. The kids want your time, not your money or better things.

Unstructured Days

Many fear the day to day drudgery of caring for kids, diapers, and toys. They see endless days that drag on and flow into one another. This could happen unless you create a structure for yourself. Get up early, exercise, read, have a set time for certain types of activities with the kids, for outings, personal hobbies, and so forth.

TAKING THE PLUNGE

Taking the plunge into the at-home world can be scary. But, in my opinion, this is worth while to those who desire it. I have heard numerous success stories of people who overcame their obstacles and quit their jobs. The rewards they received often exceeded their expectations.

*3 Keys to a Healthy Family**

1. *Parents give the family highest priority in their lives.*
2. *Quality time spent with the family produces emotional closeness.*
3. *Families have a spiritual dimension.*

*Dr. Arnold Nicholi, Jr., The Stay At Home Mom, Donna Otto, 1997

If you are going to take the plunge into the "non-working" world (which is a misnomer), you must do a few things first. Without these steps, one might give up in frustration and return to work.

- *Keep your goal at the forefront of your mind. Never forget why you are making these changes. You will need this reminder on those hard days.*

- *Live on one income before you quit. Reduce expenses as though one spouse was at home, and live like that for 3-6 months. You need to know the obstacles and also need to save for unforeseen problems down the road.*
- *Plan. Learn all you can on how to trim before you have to. Read, then read some more on the topic.*

In my first book, *Miserly Moms—Living On One Income In A Two Income Economy,* I explain how we cut our income by 50%. There are specific tips on every area of our household budget, including reducing the grocery bill to $40 per week for four people. Other books on the topic are listed in the Resource section in the back of this book.

And let us not forget the old way of doing things:

Use it up, wear it out
Make it do, do without.

CHAPTER TWO

Kids

Many persons have a wrong idea of what constitutes true happiness. It is not attained through self-gratification but through fidelity to a worthy purpose.

–Helen Keller

TEACHING KIDS FINANCIAL RESPONSIBILITY

It's no wonder the kids think money has an endless flow. They see us go to the ATM machine and withdraw any amount we want — so they think. They don't see the budgeting and planning. Some people wonder how much kids should know. Many parents have found that there are several creative ways to teach kids that the buck does stop — somewhere.

Some families involve the kids in the bill paying, letting them total the bills and seeing what's available in the checking account. Other families are not comfortable with that much exposure, so they tell them what the grocery budget is and let them total up the food bill. Managing the family entertainment budget for one month is another way some parents teach financial management. Educate your little ones on the art of balancing the budget — find something that fits your family.

Teaching through reality is the best bet, say some parents. When children have spent all of their earned money, don't let them borrow from you.

Waiting to afford something is an important lesson. Otherwise, they will love those credit cards when they arrive.

Another important question to consider — should kids get an allowance or work for their money? Many parents feel that kids need some cash and an early exposure to managing their money. Many of these same parents feel that allowances and chores should be kept separate. Since things need to be done around the house to keep it running (dishes, laundry, etc.), everyone should pitch in. Mom isn't getting paid for her chores, so why should the children?

Others feel an allowance not tied to chores is too much like welfare — they get something for nothing. They feel that earning their money prepares them for reality. These parents fear the children will feel that money is an entitlement — a dangerous attitude now and in adulthood.

Common jobs for earning an allowance

- *setting the table*
- *taking out the trash*
- *doing their own laundry*
- *sweeping kitchen floor*
- *clearing the table after a meal*
- *vacuuming or sweeping the floor*
- *making their own bed*
- *cleaning up their bedroom*

And then there are families who blend the two camps. Their kids get a small allowance and are required to work jobs for the rest of the money. This is what our family does. We have two posted lists on the refrigerator: their daily chores, and a list of jobs with a wage. Anytime a child complains of not having a something that costs, we remind them of their options.

The wage is fair for each job. We don't pay them for the job unless the job is completed. We do not withhold allowance for not doing chores, but rather withhold other privileges, like television or computer time. We believe that allowance teaches them how to handle money, and chores teach them responsibility.

Common jobs for earning extra money

- *dusting*
- *shoveling snow*
- *sweeping the walk*
- *raking leaves*
- *washing car*
- *baby sitting*
- *painting walls or fences*
- *sorting/recycling*
- *gardening*
- *mowing lawns*
- *organizing the basement*
- *word processing*
- *washing windows*
- *washing or folding family laundry*

An allowance as early as age 3 gives children something to work with. Even if you don't agree with the national average for allowances (see chart below), determine what makes you comfortable. Figure the child's expenses and go from there.

Going Rate for Weekly Allowances
(national average)

age 5	*$5*
age 7-9	*$7*
age 11-13	*$13*
age 14	*$20*

(Notice that the amount frequently coincides with the child's age)

Whether you choose to give an allowance or not, the best help you can give your children is to make a plan or budget for their needs and wants. Shockingly, very few (2%) parents require their children to have a budget. Help them write down what they have and what they hope to or need to buy. Help them see they have to make this money last all week, or they need to set aside a certain amount each week to meet that goal they have (a bike, a toy, a game ticket, gifts for others, etc.). Some parents even encourage their kids to divide their money among four categories: donation (10%), mad money for anything they want (30%), savings for smaller items (30%), big ticket item savings (30%).

Take the time to use teachable moments in the store or on outings. I have my son help at the store by asking him to find the cheapest item of what I need, or deciding if there is enough to buy that item and still go to the video store.

Other things you can do to help:

- *open a savings account for those big ticket items*
- *adopt a needy family and have everyone (parents included) donate something to them each week*
- *let the kids see you put something back because you can't afford it*
- *fix your own attitude about money: get your spending under control, stop fighting over money with your spouse, don't use credit*
- *don't pay kids for scoring on their team—you send the wrong message*
- *consider turning off the television, the commercials breed materialism in kids; they believe that they have to have that toy they see*
- *if a name brand clothing item is insisted on by the kids, let them make up the difference in price with their earned money*
- *remember that their money is their money; let them make the decisions on what to use it for, and let them live with their decisions*
- *don't give them more than you agreed upon*
- *don't withhold allowance as a disciplinary tool*

Teenagers need to start taking responsibility for their living expenses since they will soon be managing their own lives. Start giving them money for clothing, doctor bills, and whatever else you agree they should have control of. Help them set up a budget for those items, and periodically check in on their budget. Many financial counselors recommend parents still manage the payment of meals at home, shelter and utilities.

Help for younger kids

- *The Berenstain Bears Get The Gimmes* by Stan and Jan Berenstain
- *Trouble With Money* by Stan and Jan Berenstain
- *Freckle Juice* by Judy Blume
- *The Money Book: The Smart Kid's Guide to Savvy Saving and Spending* by Elaine Whatt
- *Money: Bookstore Catalog* —Lists financial books and games for all ages. Available for $2 from The National Center for Financial Education, Dept. KK, P.O. Box 34070, San Diego, CA 92163 (619) 232-8811.

Help for older kids

There is a magazine for kids that helps them think about those goodies that they see advertisements for on TV. It is put out by Consumer Reports and follows the same format: comparing and testing items for kids. This magazine appeals to ages 10-14.

Zillions: Consumer Reports For Kids
$16/year (6 issues)
P.O. Box 54861
Boulder, CO 80322
(800) 234-1645

Some parents have found that children who have no source of their own income tend to beg and nag for things they want. These kids need to have a source of money such as an allowance or job chart, so that they can budget and spend within their own means.

The most important advice parents give is to stick to whatever plan chosen. If you sometimes give in to the "gimmes" for money or toys, they won't stop when you say no. They will keep pestering you until you give in because they've seen you do it before.

LUNCH BOXES

Many folks struggle with how to provide a healthy lunch for the kids that can travel in a lunch box. Since I homeschool, I cook lunches for our kids and save a great deal. I reheat leftovers or serve something warm and inexpensive. Whenever I need to pack a lunch, I try one of the following ideas:

Main Dish:

- *tuna fish sandwich*
- *egg salad*
- *ants on a log (celery stick with peanut butter and raisins on top)*
- *bagels and cream cheese*
- *cheese and crackers*
- *lunch meat-when-on-sale sandwich (bologna, ham, turkey)*
- *peanut butter and jelly sandwich*
- *soup in a small thermos with crackers or cornbread*
- *cold pasta salad with whatever they like in it (olives, cheese chunks,*

artichoke hearts on sale, celery chunks, tofu pieces)

- *leftovers*
- *black bean sandwich spread on whole wheat bread*
- *tortilla rolled up with shredded carrot and a turkey slice*

TIP: Kids like small things so cut the sandwiches for them. Use shaped cookie cutters to make it more fun.

COOL TIP: Invest in a small freezer pack that can keep any perishable dish cold.

LEFTOVER TIP: If you make enough at dinner time to have leftovers, but the group eats everything that you make, try this tip. After the meal is made, but before you serve dinner, take the part you think should be left over, and set it aside. What they don't see they won't miss.

Snacks:

- *homemade granola bars*
- *muffins*
- *homemade cookies*
- *carrot or celery sticks*
- *popcorn*
- *homemade pudding, gelatin or rice pudding*
- *fruit*
- *applesauce*

TIP: Kids love crunchy things. Try raw veggies, pretzels, crunchy granola bars, etc. Put them in your own containers and instead of buying the prepackaged individual serving sizes.

Drinks:

Invest in a small thermos and fill it with juices bought on sale or in bulk, homemade lemonade or milk. Even reusing the pop-top water bottles makes a nice juice bottle. Avoid the prepackaged juice boxes or cans. They cost twice as much as filling a thermos.

Some people fill a water bottle half with juice and freeze. In the morning, they fill the rest of the bottle with juice. The juice stays cold all day.

Fat Content

In our fat-conscious society, many parents want their childrens' lunches to be low in fat. Often you can replace the same item for a lowfat version. For example, buy chicken or turkey hot dogs instead of full beef, or buy the more expensive fat free ones if you can. For macaroni and cheese, replace the milk with nonfat milk and the butter with yogurt. For bagel and cream cheese, buy fat-free cream cheese. Peanut butter is high in fat, but also high in protein. You don't need too much to meet a person's protein needs. The all-natural peanut butters have no added oil. For the tuna and egg salad, you can replace the mayonnaise with nonfat mayonnaise or nonfat yogurt. Disguising the taste with relish is helpful. Ham lunch meat is usually as low in fat as turkey, so watch for sales or bulk prices at warehouse clubs.

Staying within budget and fixing healthy lunches take the same planning and forethought as other meals. You can do it.

RECIPES

Here are some snack recipes to try in the childrens' lunches.

Chewy Granola Bars

2 1/4 CUPS FLOUR
1 CUP OATS (OR GRANOLA)
1/2 CUP APPLESAUCE
1/4 CUP BUTTER
1/4 CUP OIL
1 CUP SUGAR
1/2 TSP. BAKING SODA
1/2 TSP. SALT
1 EGG
2 TSP. VANILLA
1 TSP. CINNAMON
1 CUP DRIED FRUIT (RAISINS, CRANBERRIES, CHOPPED APRICOTS, DATES, ETC.)
1/2 CUP PEANUTS (OPTIONAL)

Blend the dry ingredients first, then mix with the wet. Spread in a greased 9x13 pan. Bake at 350° for 20 minutes.

Soft Pretzels

3-1/2 CUPS FLOUR
2 T. SUGAR
1 TSP. SALT
2 PKGS. (1/4 OZ.) DRY YEAST
1 CUP WATER
1 T. SHORTENING
1 EGG YOLK
1 T. WATER
COARSE SALT

In a large bowl, heat 1 cup water to 110°. Add yeast first, then all other dry ingredients. Mix well and knead for 5 minutes. Set in a greased bowl and let rise until double in size. Punch down.

Divide the dough into 12 pieces, and roll each one into a long rope (18-20 inches). Shape into pretzels or other shapes. Place on a greased cookie sheet, and rest for 5 minutes. Mix egg yolk and 1 T. water. Brush on the pretzels, then sprinkle them with the salt. Bake at 375° for 15 minutes.

FRUGAL FIVE: Lunches

$$$$$ Prepackaged foods and drinks
$$$$ Cafeteria lunch
$$$ Homemade lunch and juice box
$$ Homemade lunch with thermos of juice
$ Leftovers and thermos of juice

Frugal Five is a phrase I've coined to list five frugality choices for your family. The dollar signs ($) indicate the level of expense. The more dollar signs, the more expensive the item.

CLOTHES FOR KIDS

I spend about $350 per year on clothes for a family of four. The average American family spends more than $1000 per year. Our clothes look nice, without stains and tears. In order to spend this little, we must plan what our clothing needs will be and shop carefully. I figure how many outfits, dresses, slacks, etc. we need every month or two. I then look for the best price on these items. If I dropped into a department store without planning my shopping, I would spend $100 each time.

If buying new clothes is a hardship, but you want your children to look nice, there are some good alternatives. I have found many great bargains at the "rerun" stores throughout our area. There are the big name places, such as Savers, Salvation Army, or Goodwill. Then there are the independent thrift stores in each city. Some of the wealthier neighborhoods might have a better class of clothing to offer. There also are the seasonal resale places where a few well-organized women set up a store for a few days where people sell clothes, toys, etc. at the prices that they choose. Each of these offers some great clothes at great prices. Finding clothes may take some time, as the items come and go weekly.

Another way we get some great clothes is to exchange clothes with friends. I have friends who swap bags of outgrown clothes for their children. Some even continued after moving half way across the continent. I gladly pay a few dollars in postage for a box of clothes from my friends.

Or organize a clothing exchange at your local church or community center. Everyone drops off family member's clothing and hangs them on racks much like a department store. On the designated day, anyone in need comes and help themselves. Our church was able to clothe several families, including missionaries who needed things sent to them.

If you prefer to buy new clothes, the best way is to watch sale flyers and stock up when prices are very low. One friend taught me to save even more by buying clothes one size too large, then loosely sewing the sleeve of a shirt into the cuff, and hemming the pants. When the kids grow, let out the hems. If it's a really good sale, I buy items in their current size, plus one extra in the next size.

Garage sales and local flea markets have a lot of variety. When you see one with children's clothes and toys, stop and investigate. Again, the wealthier the neighborhood, the better quality of items. I have found nice sweaters for a dime and good toys for 1/10th their value.

FRUGAL FIVE: Clothing

$$$$$ Dropping into department stores
$$$$ Sales at department stores
$$$ Thrift stores
$$ Garage sales
$ Clothing exchanges

PETS

Kids and pets seem to go together naturally. A loving pet matched with the energy of a child can be a wonderful combination. Sometimes, however, the match isn't made in heaven. That's why it's important to make sure that the type of pet and the child are matched carefully. Most families select a pet for companionship, or because the animal is fun to watch. Knowing your family's needs and preferences will help select the right type of pet. Hopefully this section will help you own a pet on a budget without compromising its care.

If observing a pet's cute or calming behavior is a main priority, then fish, small mammals or reptiles would be the best choice. If companionship is more important, then dogs, cats or small mammals would be good selections.

Some children are rough with animals, and the parents need to make sure the pet can put up with that type of behavior. Some animals will take it well, while others will resort to bizarre behavior such as biting themselves, or perhaps biting the child. For example, a high strung lap dog would not be a good match for a rambunctious toddler.

Most families select dogs for their family pet. These are usually a great addition to the family. But before rushing out and getting one, make sure that all of the dog's needs are considered first. Are the children home enough to play with it, walk it, and love it, or are they always at after school activities? Does your family travel much? Finding care for animals while away is one of the number one complaints of pet ownership. Does the family have room for the pet? A dog needs a place to run for exercise. Most pet owners live in a house, with only 6-14% living in apartments, condominiums, or mobile homes.

Another thing to consider is whether the family can afford the animal. Expenses include the weekly food bill, the vet checkups, shots, training, etc. A dog costs an average of $13,000 during its lifetime — $4500 for food, with $3400 to vet bills. The rest is used for toys, leashes, training and housing. The average pet owner visits the pet store four-eight times per year, partly for food, but also for toys. Forty-five percent of all pet owners buy toys and gifts for their pets. Vet bills are something to factor in as well. See the chart in the "vet" section for average vet costs per family.

Another consideration is if the temperament of the desired breed matches that of the children and family. Certain types of dogs require lots of human contact and stimulation. This is especially true of Labradors and Golden Retrievers, the two most common breeds chosen for family dogs. Experienced pet owners recommend studying the different breeds that are available, paying particular attention to temperament. There are several books on breeds that are available. One highly recommended from a dog trainer is Your Purebred Puppy, by Michelle Lowell. Even though you probably won't be shopping for a pure breed, understanding how each breed tends to behave will help make a choice.

Pets Owned by People

dogs	*37%*
cats	*32%*
birds	*6%*
small mammals	*5%*
fish	*3%*
horses	*3%*

Many families start with the smaller mammals first, namely rats, guinea pigs, hamsters and rabbits. These make good starter pets as they cost very little, and the family can see how the responsibility will be handled by the children for pet ownership. Our personal favorite for pets are rats. We have had them since my son was four years old. They are surprisingly social and affectionate, even tempered, and inexpensive to purchase, feed and house (cages are small and inexpensive). If cared for well, they live up to five years.

Food

Feeding a pet is what usually deters people from owning one. If you have a ninety pound dog, he will eat as much or more than a child does. To help cut back on the expense of store bought pet food, many pet owners resort to table scraps. This is not recommended since an animal's nutritional needs differ greatly from its owners. Some people buy the cheapest brand of pet food they can with the use of coupons and sales. This may be what is necessary if the budget is strained.

Many nutritionists caution against buying cheap brands of pet food. They believe the canned food is made of diseased or old meat, but colored and flavored to look fresh. Their opinion of dry food isn't much better — filled with non-nutritious filler. There have been some studies that show that the protein in canned pet food is minimally usable to pets, with pets absorbing only 25% of the protein amount mentioned on the cans. These researchers explain that the crude protein mentioned on the label can be made from ligaments, hair, feather meal, and waste. As a result, the pets are malnourished.

These same nutritionists recommend adding raw meats and vegetables occasionally to the canine and feline diet. The pets fed this supposedly were healthier and more lively. This in turn lowered their vet bills. These experts believe that the animal's immune system cannot function if there is not some of these raw ingredients in their diet a few times per week. If you choose this approach, please research this method further. Some books on this topic are listed in the Resources section of this book.

Whether we agree with these nutritionists or not, there are some ways to avoid the high prices of pet food. One way is to make the food yourself. I am not advocating the use of table scraps for dogs or cats. This would be unhealthy for them and lead to disease and obesity in the pet. I am talking about making nutritionally balanced meals for your dog or cat.

When we lived overseas, we didn't have the luxury of canned or dry pet food, so we made our dog's food. We boiled meat bones and fresh meat scraps with rice, oil and some herbs or spices. For cats, some recommend raw oats or barley soaked in milk, with a tablespoon of oil (good for their coats) and some fresh chopped parsley. A few times a week, add some finely chopped fish or raw egg to the mixture. If these don't appeal to you, try these recipes:

Doggie Diner

Many of the recipes listed in the cat section can also be used for dogs. Here are a few others:

Vegetarian Delight (for both dogs and cats)

1/2 cup cooked rice
1/2 cup cooked corn
2 oz. tofu
1 egg yolk

Mash the tofu or dice into little bites. Mix the rest of the ingredients with the tofu. Serve.

Basic Meal

1 LB. DRY BROWN RICE
A LARGE MEAT BONE
1/2 CUP PARSLEY
WATER TO COVER
1/4 CUP OLIVE, CANOLA OR SAFFLOWER OIL

Combine all ingredients except the oil. Bring to a boil, then lower the temperature to simmer for 1 hour, or until the rice is tender. Drain excess water and add the oil. This can be refrigerated and used throughout the week.

Doggie Deluxe Hamburger

10 OZ. LEAN GROUND BEEF
1 SLICE BREAD, CRUMBLED
1 EGG
1 T. PARSLEY, CHOPPED

Combine the ingredients and form into a pattie. Broil or pan fry until done.

Good Morning Pooch

4 CUPS RICE CRISP CEREAL
2 SCRAMBLED EGGS
1 CUP PARSNIPS
1 T. OLIVE OIL

Combine in a bowl, and serve.

Dry Pet Food Recipe (cat or dog)

1 1/2 CUP WHOLE WHEAT FLOUR
1 1/2 CUP RYE FLOUR
1 1/2 CUP BROWN RICE FLOUR (GRIND DRY RICE IN BLENDER)
1 CUP WHEAT GERM
1 TSP. GARLIC POWDER
1 TSP. KELP POWDER
4 T. VEGETABLE OIL
1 1/4 CUP BEEF OR CHICKEN BROTH

After combining the dry ingredients, slowly add the oil and broth, stirring as you add. Roll the dough thinly on a cookie sheet and bake at 350° 15 minutes (or until light brown). After it is cool, break into small pieces.

Store in the refrigerator.
OPTIONS: For other flavors, add a can (15 oz.) of salmon or mackerel, or add a pound of ground chicken meat or livers to the dough before baking.

KITTY KAFE'

Kitty Salad

1 HARD BOILED EGG, CHOPPED
3 T. BOILED FISH, CHOPPED
1 TSP. MILK OR SOUR CREAM

Mix these together, and serve.

Cat Munchies

3 SALTINE CRACKERS, COOKED OATS, COOKED RICE, OR MILLET
3 T. SMOKED FISH, DICED
1 T. STEAMED VEGETABLES
1 T. SOUR CREAM, COTTAGE CHEESE, MILK OR OIL

Crumble the crackers. Mix the rest of the ingredients with the crackers. Serve.

Kitten Meal

1/3 CUP COOKED OATMEAL
2 TSP. CARROT, STEAMED AND MINCED
1 T. MEAT, MINCED
1/4 TSP. MILK, WARMED
2 TSP. WHEAT GERM OR 1 TSP. OIL

Blend all of these well in a bowl and serve.

Many cat chefs recommend that the meals be mixed with mixed vegetables, herbs and even garlic. Make sure they get some good oils (olive, safflower, etc.) in their diet. If your cat is finicky, try mixing a teaspoon of chicken fat in the food to encourage them to eat. The juice from a can of tuna poured over the food also works well.

If your cat is overweight, tripe is an excellent alternative for meat. It is fat free but high in protein.

Kittens need twice the amount of protein than an adult cat, so leave a bowl of food out at all times so they can eat throughout the day.

Feeding Small Mammals

For a small mammal, try and use the natural things in your home before resorting to the expensive bags of food sold in stores. We use the peelings from carrots and potatoes, the greens from the carrot tops, a leaf or two of lettuce, apple peelings, whole wheat bread crusts, raw oats, etc. Most of these are usually destined for the compost pile, but now have another life. And our pets love it! Our annual food bill for the rats is around $25.

What is the Biological Value of Your Pet Food?

The biological value of a food is how many of the complete amino acids the food has. Here are some protein completeness numbers:

eggs	*100%*
fish	*92%*
beef	*78%*
milk	*78%*
wheat	*60%*

These numbers assume a pure substance, without fillers (such as ligaments, hair, etc.).

VETERINARIANS

Veterinarian bills will be one of the largest expenses of owning pets. Our cat broke his leg and the x-rays and cast cost $250. If you choose one of the four–legged creatures that requires vaccinations, try and find cheaper sources than your local vet. Many pet stores host mobile vaccine clinics that run about $6-$15 per shot. One company that offers these mobile vaccination clinics is Pet Vaccine Services. To see if they service your area, call (800) 3-DOG-CAT. Another source of inexpensive vaccines is your local county Department of Animal Regulation and Control or The Humane Society.

Ways to reduce vet bills

- *keep the animal healthy through proper diet and nutrition*
- *check around for vet prices—they vary greatly*

- *use vaccine clinics for shots*
- *administer the vaccinations yourself (check feed stores or mail order catalogs)*
- *get books and videos from the library that demonstrate:*

  dental cleaning at home
  grooming
  nail clipping
  treating simple infections

Average Vet Bills Per Year

Percentage of Families	Amount Spent
32%	$150-350
29%	$ 50-150
16%	$ 350-500
12%	$500-1000
8%	$1000+
4%	less than $50

HELPFUL PET HOTLINES

For general information on treating your pet, try these hot-lines:

Hill's Pet Products..*(800) 445-5777*
Answers questions about nutrition and feeding behaviors

At Phone Vet..*(900) 988-8877*
You can speak with a veterinarian about medical and diet problems. Costs $3 per minute

Pet Lover's Helpline..*(900) 776-0007*
Recorded messages on more than three hundred topics concerning your pet. Costs $0.97 per minute. Obtain a free copy of the directory by calling the phone number

National Animal Poison Control Center..........*(800) 548-2423*
(Emergency) Charges $30 per case and accepts credit cards
or..*(900) 680-0000*
Charges $20 for the first 5 minutes of advice, then $2.95 per minute

Pet Loss Support Helpline ....(630) 603-3994
or ....(916) 752-4200
Offers counseling and support on the loss of a pet

Animal Behavior Helpline ....(415) 554-3075
Offers advice on dog and cat behavior problems

Friskies Pet Care ....(800) 366-6033
Offers advice on pet nutrition

Iams Nutrition Hotline..(800) 525-4267
Offers advice on pet nutrition

Purina ....(800) 776-7526
Offers advice on pet nutrition

On-line services are available by most internet providers. Do a search on your carrier by using keywords such as "pet forum," "animal forum," "dogs," "cats," "pet behavior," "pet training," "ask-the-vet," "reptiles," "exotic pets," "pet stories," and "pet support groups."

FLEAS

When we lived in California, the number one pest was fleas. Our vet said his main source of income came from all the flea dips and products he sold to rid our homes and pets from the little creatures. Fleas can feel like a curse. Especially if you are unable to use the chemical solutions available for this problem.

Here are some homemade remedies that worked for us when our pet and home had fleas:

For fleas and eggs in the carpets

- *Sprinkle Borax all over the carpet, especially around the edges. Work it into the carpet. Let it sit for 3 days, then vacuum.*
- *Sprinkle boric acid all around the edges of the wall. Fleas like tight places and lay eggs there. You can buy this in bulk at a hardware store (or drug store sometimes), or you can pay more and buy it at a pet store under the name of The Terminator.*

- *Sprinkle diatomaceous earth (DE) around the carpet and crevices where the wall and floor meet. This cuts their skin and dehydrates them. Don't buy the pool supply type of DE which is dangerous if inhaled.*
- *Steam clean the carpet, then vacuum daily for a few days. The hot water kills most of the eggs and fleas. The others will hatch a few days later from the heat.*
- *After vacuuming, take the bag out and seal it in a plastic bag. Set in the sun to bake the trapped fleas. I even microwaved mine for 10 seconds.*
- *Lay eucalyptus branches and leaves around the edges of the carpets in the house. It's a natural repellent, and they'll leave in a few days. Bay leaves are supposed to be effective as well.*

For fleas on the pet

- *use a flea comb, dipping it in a bowl of soapy water or rubbing alcohol after catching the fleas in the comb*
- *simmer lemons for 45 minutes, cool and strain the solution, and wet the pet thoroughly*

FRUGAL FIVE: Pet Food

$$$$$	Name brand in small packages/cans
$$$$	Generic in small packages/cans
$$$	Name brand in bulk sizes
$$	Generic in bulk sizes
$	Make it yourself

KIDS ACTIVITIES

"Hey, Mom! I'm bored! Can we go somewhere?"

These are common words in most people's homes. We have creatively found some activities that cost very little. Most take some time on Mom's part and a little creativity. There is an extensive chapter on kid's activities in my first book, *Miserly Moms*. We've found some new ones. Your kids will love the time you spend with them!

Face Paint

1 tsp. cornstarch
1/2 tsp. cold cream or Crisco
1/2 tsp. water
food coloring

Mix these together well. I divide the cream mixture into small portions, then add the food coloring of our choice to each. This way I have many colors available. I use either a paint brush or cotton swab to put it on.

Bean Bags

We take the scraps of fabric leftover from sewing and cut and sew triangles or rectangles out of them, leaving one edge open. I fill them with dry beans or sand (a plastic baggie inside will keep the sand from leaking).

Papier–Mache'

1/3 cup flour
2 T. sugar
1 c. water

Mix the flour and sugar in a pan. Add the water and mix well. Cook until clear. Don't let it boil. Cool. Pour into a shallow bowl.

Take strips of newspaper and put into the paste mixture. Rub the excess paste off of the strips and cover balloons, cardboard shapes, etc. Add several layers and then let dry. Paint if desired.

Paper Airplanes

There are many types of paper airplanes to make. My son really enjoys constructing planes, and has a few books that help with model designs and instruction. Many of the books come with paper to fold. Here are some of our favorites:

The Paper Ace, Peter Vollheim
Paper SuperPlanes, Peter Holland
The Ultimate Paper Airplane, Richard Kline
Paper Flight, Jack Botermans
Super Wings, Peter Clemens
Paper Airplanes, Emery J. Kelly

Bacteria Experiment

Watching something grow in a petri dish is interesting. But did you know you can do it at home? Little is needed to make this happen. The petri dish is the only thing that may be tricky to find. Try hobby shops, or even medical supply stores. You can use almost any replacement, as long as it is shallow, and has a lid to keep new bacteria and germs from falling inside. Everything else probably is already in your home!

4 PETRI DISHES
1/3 CUP HOT WATER
1 TSP. PLAIN GELATIN (KNOX)
1 TSP. SUGAR

Dissolve the gelatin and sugar in the hot water. When dissolved, pour into the dishes. This should be divided between four dishes.

To obtain bacteria, take one Q-tip style swab and wipe it in an area such as the inside your mouth, on the bathroom floor, between your toes, inside the sink, etc. Only one swab per area, please. Then rub the swab over the hardened gelatin inside the dish. Throw away the swab and cover the dish. Label each dish from where the bacteria came. Watch what happens during the next few days.

Make a Snow Shaker

These are the domed shakers that are filled with water and glitter and hold a scene or figure in the middle.

Making one is simple and fun. You will need:

FIGURES OR SCENERY
HOT GLUE GUN
CLEAR CAULKING
GLITTER
GLASS JAR WITH LID

Glue the figures onto the inside of the lid. Sprinkle a teaspoon of glitter into the jar and fill with water. Spread caulking around the inside of the lid. Screw on the lid tightly. Hide any caulking with a ribbon.

Lasting Bubbles

If you add a little corn syrup to your bubble soap (1 part syrup to six parts soap), then add the water, you can make bubbles that last longer before popping. We've even seen huge bubbles made using this recipe!

Modeling Dough

Kids can help mix this. Add extra fun by using rolling pins and cookie cutters. Ingredients:

1-1/2 CUPS FLOUR
1/2 CUP SALT
FOOD COLORING (OPTIONAL)
1/2 CUP WATER
1/4 CUP VEGETABLE OIL

Mix the flour and salt in a bowl. In a separate container, combine water and a few drops of food coloring. Stir the coloring to mix. Add oil to the water, then combine with the flour mixture. Mix well and knead dough until soft.

TIPS:

- *sprinkle with a little flour and knead in if dough is too sticky*
- *leftover dough can be stored in plastic bags or airtight containers to keep it soft*

Play Dough

(This is similar to the above recipe, but has a slightly different texture and lasts longer). Ingredients:

2 CUPS FLOUR
1 CUP SALT
4 TSP. CREAM OF TARTAR
2 CUPS WATER WITH FOOD COLORING
2 T. OIL

Mix together in a pan (non-stick is better). Cook on medium heat until a hard ball forms. Knead when warm for a smoother consistency.

As it becomes half-cooked, the dough is hard to mix. Keep stirring until all parts are hardened. This batch of play dough will cost only 25¢ as compared to $1.00-$3.50 for store bought.

TIPS:

- *add glitter for glitter dough when cooking is finished and you are kneading dough*
- *use unsweetened drink mix if fragrance is desired (will also add color); use 1-2 packs for each recipe*

Peanut Butter Modeling Clay

1 CUP PEANUT BUTTER
1 CUP NONFAT DRY MILK
2/3 CUP POWDERED SUGAR

Measure the peanut butter and dry milk in a large bowl and mix well. Add powdered sugar and work in with fingers. If too dry, add peanut butter. If too sticky, add dry milk. Make spiders by rolling a ball for the tummy and one for the head. Use pretzel sticks for the legs and raisins for the eyes. Or make snakes by rolling between your hands. This is a good recipe for younger kids who tend to put things in the mouth.

Street Chalk

1 CUP PLASTER OF PARIS (DO NOT PACK)
ALMOST 1/2 CUP COOL WATER
2-3 T. LIQUID ACRYLIC PAINT
SMALL PAPER CUPS

Pour plaster into a disposable container. Using a disposable stirring stick, stir in most of the water. Add paint and mix well. Add a little more water as the mixture thickens. Stir well and pour into paper cups. Peel off the paper when the chalk is dry.

Finger Paint

2 T. CORNSTARCH
2 T. COOL TAP WATER
1 CUP BOILING WATER
FOOD COLORING

Mix the cool tap water and cornstarch. Add the boiling water and stir. It should thicken as you stir. When it is cool, divide into small paper cups, or muffin tins. Then add food coloring and mix.

TIP:

- *be careful, as stains may result; stain removal ideas are in the chapter "Safer and Cheaper" of **Miserly Moms***

Quick and Cheap Finger Paint

Mix a few drops of food coloring with some shaving cream. The kids can color on paper, or in the bathtub on the tile. The bathroom is an easier place to clean.

OTHER IDEAS

- *make water balloons*
- *draw on the sidewalk*
- *go on a treasure hunt*
- *go on a scavenger hunt*
- *have a picnic (indoors or out)*
- *go to a matinee movie*
- *sponge paint on paper*

- *get funny foam at the craft store and cut shapes–decorate with puff paint*
- *do a puzzle together*
- *gather and press flowers*
- *make "edible" jewelry (string macaroni or cereal with holes in the middle)*

FRUGAL FIVE: Kids' Activities

$$$$$	Local amusement park
$$$$	Indoor play zone
$$$	Renting videos
$$	Crafts or games with the kids
$	Trip to the local park

CHAPTER THREE

Gardening

Gardening is not only an innocent and healthy, but a profitable occupation...

—Thomas Fessenden, The New American Gardener, 1828

Gardening is the number one hobby in America. But it is also a good way to cut grocery costs. I have friends who have converted their yards (back and front) of their home into a large vegetable garden. These friends grow their own produce and don't buy any at the store. One friend calculated the cost of each organic tomato that she grew at 1¢ each. That's a great savings over the store bought cost up to $1.00 each.

If you don't have a large yard, make a small garden. Many magazines have special editions on how to use a small space to produce vegetables. A four by eight foot raised garden box can produce an abundant harvest.

HOW TO START A GARDEN

For those who want to try a hand at converting their yard into a garden, here are some cost saving tips.

LOCATION

A productive garden needs at least six hours of full sun per day. Preferably, have the garden away from shrubs and trees, as they compete for water and nutrients. A gentle slope is good for cooler climates. The soil will warm faster as the sun hits it. If you have a very hot climate, a northern slope will keep the plants cooler. For bedding borders, collect rocks at a local creek.

SIZE

Any size garden is worth the effort. According to Mel Bartholomew, author of *Square Foot Gardening*, a small garden (4' x 4') can produce 32 carrots, 16 heads of lettuce, 18 bunches of spinach, 16 radishes, 16 scallions, 16 beets, 9 Japanese turnips, 5 pounds of peas, 1 head cabbage, 1 head cauliflower, and 1 head broccoli.

Look at the amount of yard needed and the yield that item will give you. For example, a zucchini bush takes up a very large area, but a pea vine does not.

Container Gardening

Don't limit yourself to the dirt on the ground. I use every space, including the fence where I grow berry vines. I also have used hanging pots to grow produce. I had a series of pots running around the eaves of my house in which I grew strawberries, carrots, lettuce, cherry tomatoes and herbs. Other plants that do well in containers are: beets, broccoli, cabbage, carrots, cucumber, eggplant, lettuce, green onions, pepper, radishes, tomatoes, zucchini, and summer squash.

The key to container gardening is proper drainage, fertilizer, sunlight and good soil. Many gardeners suggest avoiding garden soil for a container. They recommend using potting mix. You can make your own mix by combining compost or peat moss, sand and loam (equal parts).

Watering will have to be done daily since moisture cannot be retained well. If you are putting a container on the ground, make sure there is one to two inches of clearance from the ground to properly drain and to avoid rotting the bottom of the container. A container on wheels works well as it can be moved around for better sun throughout the day, and might prolong the growing season.

If you have no yard, many cities offer a community plot. There are sometimes two to three lots per city. They give you a large plot of your own, all the water you need, and free mulch for an annual fee (ours charged $60 per year). This comes to $5 per month. For fresh, organic produce, that is a bargain.

SOIL TYPE

The type of soil you have is critical to the plants' success. The pH balance and soil composition can make or break the garden. The good news is that pH can be tested. Home test kits are available at the gardening centers. Your county extension agent also is a good source for inexpensive soil testing. Often their reports will have recommendations for your soil. Soil composition also can make the seeds grow or wither. If you have clay in the soil, drainage will be a problem. For this, you need to improve the soil by mixing in organic material, compost and good soil. Sometimes even sand can be added to help drainage.

Soil Drainage

To check if drainage will be a problem, do this simple test:

Dig a hole ten inches deep. Fill it with water and let it drain. Fill it again the next day and time how long it takes to drain. If it takes longer than eight to ten hours, improve the soil.

PLANTS

Before selecting your plants, make sure they are fit for the zone you live in. Also check about micro-climates. Your city or even neighborhood may have a climate that differs from the rest of the zone. You may have more wind, cooler or hotter air, and more or less rain. Ask at nurseries or read locally written books on gardening for what grows best in your neighborhood. Also some crops are more hardy than others, and may do better in your yard.

Plant Hardiness

- *hardy plants: asparagus, beets, broccoli, cabbage, chard, carrots, kale, lettuce, onion, parsnip, peas, radish, spinach, turnip*
- *semi-hardy plants: cauliflower, potato*

- *tender plants: snap bean, sweet corn, tomato*
- *very tender plants: cucumber, eggplant, lima bean, pepper, pumpkin, squash, watermelon*

Another thing to look into is the length of growing season. In Colorado our growing season is very short, so we are limited as to what can grow here (unless we build a greenhouse).

Short season plants

bush beans, early cabbage, beets, carrots, lettuce, mustard greens, onions, peas, radishes, scallions, turnips.

Companion planting is another thing to consider. Some things go very well together while others are bad company. For example, some herbs are great to plant next to vegetables (basil will repel flies if next to tomatoes, and garlic will deter Japanese beetles near roses and raspberries). Others are not suitable (dill next to carrots will not do well). Most gardening books have a complete list of companion planting.

Companion Planting

Plant	*Deters*
basil	*flies and mosquitoes*
calendula	*most insects*
catnip	*flea beetle*
celery	*white cabbage butterfly*
flax	*potato bugs*
garlic	*Japanese beetle*
geranium	*most insects*
marigold	*Mexican bean beetle, nematodes, and other insects*
radish	*cucumber beetle*

Seeds go on sale in March at most stores. You can order through the mail by catalog. People can save their seeds after harvest. However, heirloom or non-hybrid seeds are the best to plant another crop. Be careful on storage—seeds don't like it too hot or too cold. Seeds can be bought cheaply and in the quantity you need. A list of seed sources are listed at the end of this chapter for your reference.

DISEASE AND PESTS

One of the best ways to avoid pests and disease is to keep your plants and soil healthy. Again plant crops near and around plants that deter pests.

Homemade Pesticides

- *soap sprays deter aphids (3 T. Ivory Snow or Fels Naptha to 1 gallon water)*
- *garlic or hot pepper sprays are effective on most any pest*
- *a dusting of diatomaceous earth controls aphids also*
- *place a copper band around the garden to deter snails and slugs. (This works better than stale beer in a pan or salt!)*

FERTILIZER

Feeding the plants is as important as where they grow. Certain types of plants need certain types of fertilizer. Some need nitrogen whereas others will die with nitrogen. Read up on their individual needs.

You need compost to do well at gardening. You can buy it, but making compost is easier and cheaper, and it won't stink!

How To Compost

- AREA NEEDED: *three to five cubic feet of level ground in lightly shaded area*
- BUILDING: *use wood, brick, or cement blocks; one side should be movable for access*
- AVOID: *meat, dairy, feces (cat, dog and human — other animals are okay), weeds, bones, diseased plants, needles from evergreens, eucalyptus, walnuts, charcoal, cooked food waste, dishwater, fish scraps, and grains*
- USE: *green material provides nitrogen; mix so that 50% of the material is green and alternate six inches of refuse with one inch of garden soil and green material*
- TIME: *composting will take place as soon as three weeks, but may not be ready for four months—starting in the fall is best*

- *TURNING: turning is essential to proper decomposition—if you turn it daily, you may have usable compost in three weeks*
- *TIPS: keep moist at all times, watering each layer as added*
- *READY: when the pile smells and feels like dirt, it is ready; add to soil one to two weeks before planting as it may burn the plants*

Free Stuff

- *Manure can be obtained for free from horse stables and chicken farms. Cow manure has low levels of nitrogen. Chicken manure is high in nitrogen. If using the manure in your compost pile, let it compost for several months before using to "cool it down." Often manure comes with weeds or seed, but composting before use will heat up the pile and kill the seeds.*
- *Mulch is free in some cities if they have a recycling program or a local public farm. Wood chips do not make good composting as they do not absorb water.*

WHAT ABOUT THE SURPLUS?

The main challenge of growing your own produce, or having friends who do, is the sudden surplus of one item. What do you do with 30 pounds of tomatoes all at once? One way to avoid this problem is to plant in shifts. Plant one row one week, another the next week, etc. so that they ripen in shifts as well. If you are the recipient of bushels of produce from generous friends, there are ways to stretch the produce to last all year. Remember that our farming ancestors learned this art. That's how they had food all year round. Preserving is done by salting, pickling, canning, freezing, and drying. I recommend looking into these for your family if you have abundance of any food item. You won't buy that food item most of the year.

To preserve my bounty, I bake a bunch of meals or snacks from that one food item to freeze. I make jam, zucchini bread, tomato sauce or whatever I have. I then have what I need all year. Below are some tips that are mainly for excess zucchini, pumpkins, tomatoes and fruits (they are the most commonly grown in home gardens). More tips for storage and recipes for using excess crops can be found in my first book, *Miserly Moms.*

Zucchini Relish

7 ZUCCHINI, CHOPPED UNPEELED
4 LARGE ONIONS, CHOPPED
1 LARGE SWEET RED PEPPER, CHOPPED
1 CAN (4 OUNCES) CHOPPED GREEN CHILIES
3 T. SALT
3-1/2 CUPS SUGAR
3 CUPS VINEGAR
1 T. GROUND TURMERIC
4 TSP. CELERY SEED
1 TSP. PEPPER
1/2 TSP. GROUND NUTMEG

Combine first five ingredients and let rest overnight. The next day, rinse the relish and drain. Bring the remaining ingredients to a boil. Add relish to the pot and simmer. While it's hot, put into jars. Leave a small space at the top. Fit lids on tight. Follow proper canning procedures for sealing if relish is to be stored.

Zucchini Bread

3 EGGS, BEATEN
1-1/2 CUPS SUGAR
1/4 CUP OIL
1/2 CUP CONCENTRATED APPLE JUICE
3 TSP. VANILLA
3 CUPS GRATED ZUCCHINI
3 CUPS FLOUR
1 TSP. BAKING SODA
4 TSP. BAKING POWDER
1 TSP. SALT
3 TSP. CINNAMON
1/2 TSP. NUTMEG
1/2 TSP. ALLSPICE

Combine the above ingredients and mix well. Pour in greased and floured full-sized, loaf pan and bake at 350° for fifty to sixty minutes. Remove from the oven and cool before slicing.

Other good uses for zucchini are zucchini and potato pancakes and spaghetti sauce with zucchini.

TOMATO TIPS

- *select firm tomatoes with dark color; they should feel heavy as light tomatoes can be mealy and bland*
- *keep at room temperature*
- *very ripe tomatoes should be refrigerated*
- *if you have unripened tomatoes on the vine and frost is imminent, pull up the whole vine and hang upside down in a cool dark place; they will ripen slowly over a few weeks*
- *when cooking fresh tomatoes, avoid aluminum pans—the acid in the tomatoes may react and form an unpleasant taste*
- *in cooked tomato dishes, a pinch of sugar helps the flavor*
- *wash tomatoes right before use—washing before storage can cause spoilage*
- *to peel a tomato, place in boiling water for thirty seconds, then into cold water, and the skin will come right off*
- *freeze unneeded tomatoes whole and when fully ripened*
- *dry tomatoes by using the recipe below*

How to sun dry a tomato

6 LBS. RIPE TOMATOES (PREFERABLY ROMA-LESS WATERY)
2 T. SALT
3 CUPS OLIVE OIL

Preheat oven to 200°. Slice tomatoes lengthwise and arrange on racks or screens. Sprinkle with salt. Bake until 3/4 their original size with no signs of moisture. This will take eight to nine hours. Remove from oven and cool one hour. Pack in pint-size jars and cover completely with oil. Seal tightly. Store up to eight weeks.

Salsa

1 T. OLIVE OIL
2 ONIONS, DICED
2 CLOVES GARLIC, MINCED
1 GREEN PEPPER, DICED
1 RED PEPPER, DICED
2-3 CUPS DICED FRESH TOMATOES
3 TSP. WINE VINEGAR
1/4 TSP. BLACK PEPPER
1 T. FRESH CILANTRO, CHOPPED
1/4 TSP. CAYENNE PEPPER OR JALAPENO PEPPERS

(These proportions can be varied to suit taste.)

Heat oil and sauté onion, garlic, green pepper, and red pepper. Add tomatoes, and rest of ingredients to pan and stir. Remove from heat immediately. Serve with tortilla chips or on top of refried beans or corn bread.

APPLES

When my mom's apple tree is in season, we have lots of great apples. We eat the best, and store the rest by making applesauce (boil down and mash with a fork), cobbler, and apple butter, or freezing (put pieces in plastic bags ready for pie at any time) or drying (thinly slice and lay on baking sheet overnight at 200°).

BERRIES

Growing your own berries is the best way to enjoy these lovely fruits. When a berry is vine ripened, it is so much sweeter than any store bought version. If you cannot grow your own, visit a local farm that allows you to pick your own fruit. We visit a berry farm that is 40 miles away. Many question the cost savings with the gas used in driving. The day is a fun outing for the family as we enjoy the fresh farm air together. The raspberries and strawberries that we picked were 75% less expensive than what the stores sell. We made jam and cobblers that lasted for months. Making jams are the best way to use up some extra fruits before they spoil. Frozen fruit pops, fruit leather, and fruit juice also are great uses for extra fruit.

Homemade Fruit Juice

Cook the fruit in a large kettle with very little water added. Drain the juice, and add one cup of sugar to each quart of juice. Boil, then skim any foam. Pour in bottles and seal with paraffin wax. This works with grape, cherry, apple, plum, and most fruits.

Cranberry Sauce

After Thanksgiving, fresh cranberries go on sale. Buy several bags of these to make into juice or jelly. They can be frozen for up to a year.

1 BAG CRANBERRIES
8 OZ. FROZEN CONCENTRATED APPLE JUICE

Simmer together for 5 minutes and refrigerate.

GETTING HELP

Sometimes we need help in our gardening efforts. Check with your county extension agent. Occasionally a nursery worker offers great advice. Help at our fingertips, is available also.

Online gardening

The Internet provides discussion with other gardeners, reference material, mail-order supplies and even pictures of plants and gardens. If you have access to online servers, there are several types of groups that can help. There are groups set up by the server for its members only. There are user groups (often called "lists") that you subscribe to and are sent a list of comments and discussions that members write in. And then there are websites set up as references.

Here's some help on how to find gardening help that your server has set up for you. Once you log onto the server, try entering keywords such as:

gardening
garden
home and garden
garden club
horticulture
landscape
plants
agriculture
herbs
master gardener
chili heads

There are many gardening lists (or discussion groups) to subscribe to. I have chosen a few for gardeners who want to grow vegetables. Here are some addresses to try:

GENERAL GARDENING INFORMATION
listserv@ukcc.uky.edu

HOBBY GREENHOUSES
listserv@ulkyvm.louisville.edu

MEDICINAL HERBS
listserv@trearnpc.ege.edu.tr

AROMATIC AND MEDICINAL HERBS
listserv@vm3090.ege.edu.tr

CHILE LOVERS
listserv@chile.ucdmc.ucdavis.edu

To subscribe to any of these lists, just send a one line message, asking for a sample copy of the digest.

Websites

Websites are fun to check out because they can offer so much information on a few pages. Here are some that are helpful:

AGRICULTURE
http://agcomwww.tama.edu/agcom/agrotext/visitor.html

MIDWESTERN GARDENING
http://www.prairienet.org/ag/garden/homepage.htm

GENERAL GARDENING BULLETIN BOARD
http://www.gardenweb.com

GARDENING RESOURCES
http://www.olympus.net/gardens/welcome/html

Other websites for specific seed companies are listed below, under their name.

Seed Sources

(and this is just a few of what's out there!)

BURPEE
032763 Burpee Building, Warminster, PA 18974
Phone: 800-888-1447 Fax: 1-800-487-5530

CORNS
Phone:405-778-3615

CYBERSEEDS.COM
Xeriscape Seed, tropical seeds, exotic seeds, cacti seeds, grass seeds
PO Box 171102, San Antonio, TX 78217-1102
Fax: 1-888-466-3320
http: //www.cyberseeds.com

FOREVER SUMMER HYDROPONICS
Suppliers of the cheapest artificial growing equipment in the UK and possibly the world!
Phone: 01242 255622
30 Hewlett Road Cheltenham, Glos GL52 6AA England
http: //www.foreversummer.demon.co.uk

GARDENSALIVE!
Source for organic garden products (& lawn seed)
Phone: 812 537-8650 Fax: 812 537-5108
E-mail: 76375.2160@compuserve.com

HIGH COUNTRY GARDENS
Water wise plants
Phone: 800-925-9387 Fax: 1-800-925-0097

JOHNNY'S SELECTED SEEDS
310 Foss Hill Rd.
Albion, Maine 04910
207-437-4301
http:// www.johnnyseeds.com/

LE JARDIN DU GOURMET
The .25 cent seed packet!
Phone: 802-748-1446 Orders: 800-659-1446 Fax: 802-748-9592
E-mail: Flowers.Herbs@Kingcom

PARK SEED COMPANY
Cokesbury Rd.
Greenwood, S.C. 29647
Phone: 800-845-3369
http://www.parkseed.com/

SANTA BARBARA HEIRLOOM SEEDLING NURSERY
Phone: 805-968-5444

SEEDS OF CHANGE ORGANICALLY GROWN SEEDS
Phone: 888-762-7333 Fax: 888-Fax-4SoC (329-4762)
http: //www.seedsofchange.com

SHEPHERD'S GARDEN SEEDS
Phone: 860-482-3638 Fax: 860-482-0532
E-mail: garden@shepherdseeds.com
http: //www.shepherdseeds.com/

SIMPSON'S HERB FARM
Culinary, medicinal and ornamental herb seeds for the gardener, cook, crafter and herbalist
Phone Orders: 501-456-2740 Fax Orders: 501-456-2792
http: //www.simpsonsherbfarm.com

TEA HERB FARM
Phone: 573-437-3053
Rt. 1, Box 71,Tea, MO 63091-9714
http: //mvpimages.net/teaherbfarm

TERRITORIAL SEED CO.
P.O. Box 157, Cottage Grove, OR 97424-0061
Phone: 541-942-9547 Fax: 888-657-3131
http: //www.territorial-seed.com

TOTALLY TOMATOES
Phone: 803-663-0016

More Seed Companies

If the above list wasn't enough, these websites have lists of seed and plant companies:

http://www.cog.brown.edu/gardening/cat16/frame-cat.html
http://pbmfaq.dvol.com/list/

For a comprehensive list of seed-selling companies, check out the following book at the library—*Gardening By Mail,* by Barbara Barton, *1997.*

CHAPTER FOUR

Fun In The Sun Vacations

I'm sorry ma'am, but I'm afraid that your husband doesn't qualify as a carry-on item.

–McPherson cartoon

You or your spouse have slaved away for a long time without a break and you need a vacation. You're ready to head to the beach or mountains or desert (or all three, if you live in California).

The first thing you may want to ask yourself is, why am I taking a vacation? There may be any number of reasons. The most obvious is to get away from work and recharge your batteries—to relax with a good book, soak up some rays, or do a little body surfing or boogie boarding.

Vacations can also be a wonderful time of family bonding. Spending time with each other without the pressures of jobs, schoolwork, housework, lawn work, cooking, laundry, and lots of other chores can reveal new or previously unknown personality quirks, traits, and characteristics.

During vacation, you can explore areas of the country that you've never visited before. Many people from the East or Midwest, for example, are astounded by the beauty and grandeur of the American West (although some of its impact has often been mitigated by prior visual images from postcards and TV).

In any case, vacations are meant to be times of refreshment and relaxation. But how often have we experienced just the opposite? Chevy Chase practically made a whole career out of the holidays-gone-amuck theme with his various vacation movies.

NECESSITY OF PLANNING

The single most important aspect to having a successful vacation is planning. Without careful planning, a vacation can turn into a living nightmare. Murphy's Law — whatever can go wrong, will — seems to be especially operative when it comes to vacations. A carefully planned vacation doesn't mean, however, that there isn't any room for spur-of-the-moment activities. A side trip to the Painted Desert or St. Augustine or a Civil War battle site can sometimes prove to be the highlight of an entire vacation. However, these unplanned excursions need to occur within an already carefully planned vacation schedule.

Planning is essential to any type of vacation, whether it's a simple weekend spent in a tent, or a month traveling throughout the Southwest. In some ways, the simpler — or, perhaps, the more frugal — the vacation, the more planning is needed. For example, tent camping, one of the most economical kinds of vacation, can require the most planning. There are literally hundreds of details that need to be taken care of.

Some details to consider are:

- *How will you get to your destination? If you are flying, where will you leave your car?*
- *Where will you eat along the way? Will you take a cooler for most meals and save the restaurant expense?*
- *Will you pack less clothing than you need — and use laundromats?*
- *Will you look for a motel with a kitchen so you can save on restaurant meals?*
- *Have you made a list of items to bring so nothing gets left out? Some travel books have starter lists that you can add to.*

Before You Leave...

- *have your mail and newspaper picked up daily by a neighbor or friend (having it stopped alerts some people to the fact that you are gone)*
- *have a neighbor watch for parcels or packages that may be left at your door*
- *leave a phone number with a friend or neighbor where you can be reached in case of emergency*
- *turn off your water heater and thermostat before leaving*
- *put any perishables in the freezer instead of leaving them in the refrigerator*

How Long to Stay?

An important consideration when planning a vacation is to think about how long you want to stay. A "vacation" can be anything from a weekend to months. Typically, it is two or three weeks in the summer. American companies are usually less generous with vacation time than their European counterparts — which often give workers a month or more off.

Many families have found that three weeks is just about ideal for a family summer vacation. You spend the first week adjusting to the fact that you are in a different place with a different routine. The second week is generally the high point. You've acquired the vacation mind set, your burn is turning to tan, and you don't have a care in the world. Some time during the third week the reality that your vacation is about to end starts to set in. The tendency here, which should be resisted, is to try to squeeze every single last bit of enjoyment out of the remaining days. This is usually a formula for frustration and despair. Better to sit back, relax, and let the remaining days go by with as little thought to their ending as possible.

Most of us, however, only can take one week for a vacation. When we had zero money, we spent our vacation camping. For a few dollars a night, we could enjoy the outdoors and go hiking, swimming, or fishing. We drove up the coast of California and visited the beauty of northern California — a different spot each day. One word of caution though: we found a week of camping to be too long. We tired of the uncomfortable beds, dirt in our clothes, and poor clean up facilities. Make sure you can handle that much "roughing it" before you plan on it for that long of a period of time.

Mini-vacations also can be very refreshing. This could be anything from a night downtown or a long three-day weekend. Many hotels and resorts offer special prices for these mini-stays, and you can often get special airfares if you have a flexible schedule and can leave at the drop of a hat. I know families that take several three-day weekends throughout the year instead of one long vacation.

TYPES OF VACATIONS

What pops into your mind when you think of a vacation? If you've been watching any TV, it's probably a romantic getaway to a secluded South Seas island, or a cruise through the Caribbean. These are, of course, classic images of vacations. But for the frugal family, a vacation of this type is probably not a reality: they're just too expensive.

There are lots of really relaxing and fun vacations that couples and families can enjoy together that don't put a major crimp in the budget. Some of these include the following: tent camping, staying in a cabin, borrowing or renting a motor home from a friend, renting a vacation home, exchanging a home with someone in another part of the country or in a foreign country, vacation packages, vacationing during the off season, and even traditional motel vacationing.

When picking the type of vacation to have with children involved, it will go smoother if you keep a few tips in mind. First, plan the trip with your kids, but not around your kids. Their interests should be considered in the planning, but don't let them dictate what type of trip you have. Involve them in the planning, and go over brochures and pictures with them. Secondly, even though you will be doing most of the planning, allow for spontaneous side trips that would appeal more to the kids than you. Third, avoid long bus or car rides. If you need to travel for a long period, take breaks. Fourth, allow for "down time," or play time each day. Fifth, make sure snacks and rest stops are planned in to the daily schedule. Sixth, with children of different ages and interests, occasionally divide up into groups and see different things.

Tent Camping

Let's face it. Not everybody likes to camp. But it yields some wonderful family expeditions, and a wonderful experience of the great outdoors.

One of the greatest pleasures of camping is experiencing nature up close and personal. Few things are more exhilarating than coming out of a tent on a crisp summer morning to behold one of the incredible vistas that one often encounters when camping. And, there's nothing quite like a meal cooked over a campfire after a long day of hiking or fishing.

Another thing to remember is that, somewhat perversely, there seems to be an inverse relationship between the beauty of the campsite and the quality of the hygienic facilities. We have found that invariably the best camp grounds are equipped with what are euphemistically called "vault facilities," which is nothing more than a hole in the ground with some kind of structure over it (these used to be called "outhouses"). Some of the best campsites can be found in the National Forest Service system. These camps typically are the most beautiful, least expensive — and most primitive. Don't expect hot showers and fancy plumbing. Some even lack running water. Often, the more uncivilized the more sensational the views.

Planning – the Key to Successful Camping

While planning is usually necessary for any vacation, it is absolutely essential for camping. The first thing to decide is where to camp. I enjoy camping out West. I know that there are many lovely places to camp in other regions, but since most of my experience comes from camping in the West, let me explain why I like it so much. A number of factors contribute to this, among them scenery, weather, and availability and diversity of campgrounds.

It's almost as if the West is set up to be camped in. Perhaps the most notable thing about camping out West is the spectacular scenery. The mountains of Colorado, the national parks of southern Utah, the deserts of the Southwest, the redwoods and beaches of California — all provide breathtaking vistas. The sights, the sounds, and the smells are often amazing. There's nothing quite like waking up in a pine forest, or hiking through the desert in springtime, or hearing the gentle murmur of surf or smelling the tangy salt of the ocean.

Weather out West also is ideal for camping. Typically, at any elevation, summer in the West will feature bright, sunshine days and cool, crisp nights that are ideal for sleeping. Even the regions of the West that experience late-afternoon thunderstorms generally clear up by the evening and leave behind crystalline skies and the most delightful crisp scent one could imagine. If you do camp out West, even in the summer, be prepared for nighttime temperatures as low as the upper thirties.

Check your local library or bookstore for books that list and describe the features of these campgrounds. You'll want a book that tells you such things as the relative beauty of the setting, number and size of actual sites, special features about particular sites, proximity to adjacent sites, access to the campground (easy or difficult), facilities, nearby activities, quality of hiking trails, availability of fishing/hunting, and how to reserve a site. Be sure you know the reservation policies well in advance of when you actually plan to be there because some of the more popular campgrounds fill up months ahead of actual occupancy. Two of my favorite travel books that offer all of this information are *Family Travel,* and *Free Vacations and Bargain Adventures in the USA,* both by Evelyn Kaye.

There are also many beautiful private, state, and national park campgrounds. The private camping areas can be more expensive. The public areas of the state and national parks tend to be more crowded and not quite as scenic.

Before venturing with the tent, plan and prepare—it will help make the trip more enjoyable. Below are some main items to consider, but for a more thorough list, check a camping guide book.

Things to check for:

- *bug repellent for insects*
- *adequate padding under your sleeping bag (test by sleeping on it before leaving)*
- *rain gear for surprise cloudbursts*
- *practice putting up and tearing down the tent in the backyard*
- *plan for protecting your food and gear from curious animals (keeping it locked in the car is helpful)*
- *be ready for the ripe fragrances that waft from bodies unwashed for days on end*

Our experience is that something special often happens when we tent camp. Few of us have the opportunity to experience the beauties of creation on a regular basis. Getting away from life in the city or suburbs and out into nature can be tremendously restorative.

Motor Home Camping

Another way to have a relatively inexpensive vacation is to borrow or rent a friend's motor home. This, of course, presupposes a) that you have friends, b) that at least one of them has a motor home, and c) that they'll let you use it. I don't have first-hand knowledge about all the protocol associated with actually obtaining a borrowed motor home, but I have heard that this usually comes about as a result of the friend telling a select circle of friends that such vehicle is available for their use. In other words, the friend initiates the conversation about the availability of his motor home, not you.

If you do indeed obtain use of such a vehicle, remember that motor home camping is quite different that tent camping. For example, the number of campgrounds is smaller, as well as the number of motor home sites within campgrounds. You are also one step removed from nature (which can be good or bad). The vehicle itself will "guzzle" gas. You cannot make as good time on the road. You will find yourself transformed into the guy everyone hates who has traffic backed up for miles as you struggle to make it up the mountain on that two lane road.

Nevertheless, there are still plenty of spectacular motor home camping opportunities, and the people who have them usually recommend them highly.

Renting a Vacation Home

Believe it or not, renting a vacation home can be quite reasonable. We know a family of eight that has gone to the same vacation area on the East Coast for nearly twenty years. Each year they rent a beach house, and (as this is being written) are still able to get one for under $500 a week. If you look hard enough, you can still find bargains. If you are interested in a specific city, check out the phone books for that city at your local library. You can also call the chamber of commerce in that city and ask for a listing of all vacation rentals in the area.

Relatives or Friends

One time-tested way to reduce vacation costs is to stay at the home of friends or relatives. If you live in Illinois and have relatives or friends in Colorado, perhaps they will invite you to visit them. This can make for a pleasant enough vacation, provided several things are in place.

First, have they really made it clear that you're welcome? Sometimes people will offer to have you visit them not really expecting you to take them up on it. If they offer, check it out thoroughly with them. Plan the time in advance so they can prepare.

Second, don't stay too long. Remember, fish and relatives begin to stink after a few days. It's probably better to have a stay at a friend or relative's house be part of a larger vacation plan, where you spend, say, only three days out of two weeks there. An extended visit by a large number of people can place a tremendous burden on a family.

Third, be genuinely grateful for the opportunity to stay there, and find a way to express your gratitude beyond a thank-you note (which you should always send). One way is to offer to take them out to dinner—probably without the kids (too much hassle, especially with two large families). Or perhaps you could offer to pay for an excursion to a nearby national park or monument.

Motel Vacations

It is not out of the question for families to plan reasonably-priced vacations and stay in motels. Once again, the key is planning in advance. If you book rooms far enough ahead, you can sometimes save 10 to 20% even during peak seasons. Shop around in advance. Go to the library or a bookstore, get the best travel guide for your vacation area, copy down names and numbers of places to stay that look interesting, call, write, or e-mail them for a brochure, and then do a little comparison pricing. Brochures can be very helpful because they not only give you complete descriptions of facilities but also give you full-color pictures of the motel, its rooms, lounges, and the surroundings. Sometimes this can be misleading, but, when combined with guidebook recommendations, it generally pays off.

To get the best discount on a room, talk with a supervisor or hotel manager. They make pricing decisions. If you are using the toll-free number for a chain hotel, call the individual hotel directly to see if they can do better. Sometimes they are hungry for business and will offer better prices. Also use any travel club discounts that you might have (such as AAA — Automobile Association of America or AARP — American Association of Retired Persons).

The day of the week can also effect the price you pay. Some more popular spots will be busier on the weekends, and may offer lower mid-week rates. The same goes for season and off-season periods. Some off-season periods are just fine for weather, and are less crowded.

Other Housing Options

For the more adventurous and flexible, there are some other options for housing. College dormitories rent out the rooms in the summer. Some are as low as $15 per night. To get a list of the campuses that participate, buy a book called *Campus Lodging*, or contact:

THE CAMPUS TRAVEL SERVICE
P.O. Box 5486
Fullerton, CA 92635
(800) 525-6633
http://www.campus-lodging.com

Stay at the YMCA. To see if one of their 40 nationwide locations is near your destination, contact:

THE Y'S WAY
224 E. 47th Street
New York, NY 10017
(212)308-2899
http://www.ymca.org

Check out the youth hostels (or elder hostels if you are a senior citizen). They cost on average $10 per night:

AMERICAN YOUTH HOSTELS
1017 K Street, NW
Washington D.C. 20001
202-783-6161

ELDERHOSTELS
75 Federal Street
Boston, MA 02110-1941
(617-426-8056)
http://www.elderhostel.org

When thinking about lodging, it is a good idea to think about it as a headquarters. For example, a motel in Durango, Colorado, is a good headquarters or base, for exploring the high desert, Four Corners area. Santa Fe would make a good base for the New Mexico highlands, and Sedona, Arizona, for the desert Southwest. Northern Arkansas would be an ideal spot for touring the Ozarks, Missouri, and the beauty there. Or, you could just stay put in any one of those places. All of them have lots to do.

House Swapping

One way to vacation at a very low price is to swap your residence.

Exchanging homes can save you the single highest cost of vacationing — the money you pay to stay somewhere. It also can save on food because it is much cheaper to do your own cooking than to eat out.

For those who are serious about house swapping, there are organizations to help put you in touch with other house swappers. You pay an annual fee that ranges from $25-75 to list a description of your home in a catalog that goes to other members several times a year.

If one or several of the listings look interesting, you contact the people and provide details about your own home, its location, and possible swap dates. Potential house swappers will also contact you. It is good to send letters of inquiry at least six months in advance.

Details such as paying utilities, pet care, car use, and lawn care can be negotiated. It is wise to put these agreements in writing. Though not legal documents, they can help avoid misunderstandings. The following are addresses for home swapping services:

HomeLink U.S.
P.O. Box 650
Key West, FL 33041
(800) 628-3841
E-mail: homelink@conch.net
Listings: 15,000, published five times a year
Cost: $78 to list your home

Intervac
30 Corte San Fernando
Tiburon, CA 94920
(415) 435-3497
E-mail: intervacUS@aol.com
Listings: 10,000 published four times a year
Cost: $78 to list your home plus $11 to include a photo of your home

International Home Exchange Network
P.O. Box 915253
Longwood, FL 32791
(407) 862-7211
Website: http://www.ihen.com
Listings: Allows non-members to view all listings

Trading Home International
P.O. Box 787
Hermosa Beach, CA 90254
(800) 877-TRADE
Website: http://trading-homes.com
Listings: Currently has 1,445 listings

Home Stays

Similar to house swapping, a home stay involves living in someone else's home. The major differences are 1) that you actually stay together with the host family, and 2) it always involves staying in a foreign country. The concept grew out of student exchange programs and has now been extended to families and other groups of adults.

The primary appeal of home stays is that you get a much deeper understanding of a foreign culture by staying in someone's home than by staying in a motel. Having never experienced a home stay, I can nevertheless think of lots of drawbacks — language difficulties, little or no privacy, few opportunities to "just hang out and relax", plenty of opportunities for major cultural faux pas. But if you're adventurous, a home stay might be just the thing for you. Here are some addresses for home stay sources:

American-International Homestays
P.O. Box 1754
Nederland, CO 80466
(800) 876-2048

Services: Places travelers with English-speaking hosts in 29 countries.

AmeriSpan
P.O. Box 40513
Philadelphia, PA 19106
(800) 679-6640
Website: http://www.amerispan.com

Services: Arranges language study and home stays at more than 35 schools in 12 Latin American countries.

Elderhostel
75 Federal St.
Boston, MA 02110-1941
(617) 426-7788
Website: http://www.elderhostel.org

Services: Combines home stays with non-academic courses and field trips. Two-to four-week programs in 10 international countries. For those age 55 and older.

Friendship Force
(Takes all requests via telephone)
(800) 688-6777

LEX AMERICA
68 Leonard St.
Belmont, MA 02178
(617) 489-5800
Website: http://www.lexlrf.com

Services: Arranges home stays for adults, families, and students in Japan and Korea. Also arranges opportunities for U.S. families to host foreign visitors.

SERVAS
Suite 407, 11 John St.
New York, NY 10038
(212) 267-0252
Website: http://servas.org

Services: produces a directory providing descriptions of 14,000 home stay opportunities in 135 countries. A $25 deposit enables you to borrow a country list and make your own arrangements. An application, letters of recommendation, and an interview are required to join. Membership is $55.

WORLD LEARNING
(FORMERLY EXPERIMENT IN INTERNATIONAL LIVING)
Seventh floor, 419 Boylston St.
Boston, MA 02116
(800) 662-2967
Website: http://www.worldlearning.org

Services: One-to four-week home stays in 22 countries following an application and letters of recommendation.

Overseas Travel Tips

- *drink only bottled water with a seal that you must break in order to open**
- *drink only sodas that come in cans or bottles (no fountain sodas)*
- *don't drink anything with ice in it*
- *don't rinse your toothbrush under the faucet—use your bottled water*
- *don't eat fresh vegetables or fruits (unless the skin is peeled off by you); the water used to wash them can be contaminated*
- *avoid raw or undercooked meats, shellfish, or fish*
- *if you get "the crud," drink plenty of fluids*

*Author's note: I specifically mention the *seal* because of an incident we had on an overseas trip. We asked for bottled water to be put in our rooms for teeth brushing and drinking. One afternoon we returned early and found the maid filling our bottled water containers from the tap!

Vacation Clubs

Have you ever gotten a call from a "travel agent" offering you four days and three nights free in some semi-exotic place like Myrtle Beach, Orlando, or Tucson? All you have to do is attend a short "presentation" and collect your free vacation. When you show up, the "presentation" turns out to be a hard-sell sales pitch to sign up for 5, 10, or 20 years of vacations at special discounted prices. Yes, you can pick up your free vacation without buying anything, but not until you've been told you're an idiot in no uncertain terms if you don't sign up for one of the packages. If you end up not taking the bait, be prepared to be treated like a pariah, a scoundrel, a fool.

The package deals themselves will save you money in the long run, if you are already in the habit of taking fairly expensive vacations in places like the West Indies, Bermuda, or Cancun, and if you have a large chunk of change to plunk down. If you don't have the cash handy and have to finance the outlay (which will be thousands of dollars), you will probably end up losing. We have friends who have signed up for these packages who are satisfied that they've gotten a good deal, but they're not really in the same tax bracket as we are.

Flying vs. Driving

OK. You know where you want to go, everyone's excited, but how do you get there? Drive or fly? Of course, if you're going to Bermuda it's a little difficult to get there by car. But what if you're going from St. Louis to Santa Fe? You could easily drive it in two days (one, if you're a real road warrior). Or, you could fly into Albuquerque, rent a car, and drive there. Unless you are a travel agent (where you can save up to 75%), work for the airlines (where you can get free flights for you and your family), or have many frequent flyer miles saved, driving probably will be a lot cheaper, especially if you have a large family traveling.

A good way to save money if you're driving to your vacation is through coupon books. These are available for free at rest areas along major interstates. They usually contain discount coupons for food, lodging, and other travel expenses. Motels, looking to fill rooms that would otherwise go empty, offer substantial discounts off regular rates. It is wise to call ahead and reserve the room using the coupon. They'll advise then if they are full.

Usually there are at least two or three participating motels at each exit, so you should find something to meet your family's needs.

Quite a few people, however, don't like to drive long distances. For a large family, driving to a vacation requires owning or obtaining a suitable vehicle such as a minivan or a sport utility vehicle (SUV). Unfortunately, these vehicles are expensive to own or rent, especially an SUV. They also aren't typically very comfortable for long distance driving. Think about swapping cars with someone who owns one of these vehicles. Of course, you'll have to verify auto insurance coverage.

Airline Travel

There are ample opportunities to save money on airline travel. Savings can involve the use of discount travel agencies, frequent flyer coupons, vouchers sold at grocery stores and even the Internet.

Travel agencies have been snubbed by many frugal travelers because they don't want to pay the agency's commissions. There are, however, many great deals that discount travel agencies can offer. The difference between a discount travel agency and a regular travel agency is that the discount agency has little to no overhead (no office, no receptionist, no glitzy ads). Sometimes the discount agencies add to the savings by buying up blocks of seats at a low price and pass on the savings to us. Watch the newspaper for ads in the travel section for discount agencies. Here are a few of those that buy blocks of seats and offer good discounts:

UniTravel Corp. .... *(800) 325-2222*
TFI Tours Intl. .... *(800) 745-8000*
1-800-FLY-CHEAP .... *(800) 359-2432*
Airhitch .... *(212) 864-2000*

Other types of agencies that offer good deals are through travel clubs such as AAA. They offer low fares on airlines as well as cruises, hotels and trains. They also offer reasonable rates on package deals for destinations such as Alaska, Disneyland, and Disney World. To check out their travel services (if you are a AAA member) call 800-272-2155 or check their website at *http://www.csaa.com*

Ever consider buying an airline ticket with your broccoli? That's becoming more popular these days. Airlines are teaming up with grocery stores and offering travel vouchers with a certain grocery total. This can be a great source of savings on airline tickets. With these vouchers, we were able to fly for less than it would have cost us to drive.

One of the most helpful areas for saving on airline travel comes from the Internet. It can provide the lowest prices with the least amount of time invested to find them. There are also quite a few free travel websites as well as newsletters that you can subscribe to and receive over the Internet (these are listed at the back of this chapter). You can even make your reservations for most airlines, hotels, and car rentals via the Internet. Of course, as with any use of the Internet, do use caution. I never give my credit card number over the Internet, but rather call after I have obtained the price I saw on the net, the flight number, date and time.

Several websites have been set up for easy access to low fares and many choices. One of my favorites is offered by Excite at *http://city.net/forms/reservations*. This website asks you what cities you want to travel between, what date, what time of day, and then lists the ten cheapest fares on all airlines. You can adjust the dates and times to see if it effects the price. For example, by flying on Thanksgiving morning instead of Wednesday night (the night before), you can save a bundle. I have never found a cheaper fare by calling agencies or airlines directly. Another one of my favorite Internet sites is Arthur Frommer's web site *(http://www.frommers.com)* where he has an encyclopedia of information about any kind of travel you can imagine.

Another excellent use of the Internet for airline travel is the excess seats offered at super cheap fares for domestic and international travel. Basically, the airlines are trying to sell seats that would otherwise go unsold—so any money is better than no money, and you benefit too! These savings can range from 30%-75% off regular fares.

Below is a list of five of the major airline carriers who offer this service. Some are very easy to subscribe to — some are a little more complex. All five of the airlines listed below offer this service free. Here's how it usually works. You subscribe once, and then every Monday through Wednesday you will receive an e-mail with the Internet airfare specials. All but Northwest automatically e-mail your address. For Northwest you must go to their website on Wednesday and check the fares.

Some carriers send you every special they offer. For other carriers you can be more specific when you register and select departure and destination cities. Then these airlines only will send you notice of specials for the cities you selected. You also can call their 800 numbers on Wednesdays to hear what cheap seats are available.

The catch on these savings is that most require departure on the next Friday or Saturday and return on Sunday, Monday, or Tuesday. Some are more flexible with scheduling. There also is a limit as to which cities these offers are extended to. Sometimes international fares are offered for less than most regular domestic fares. If you can be flexible, spontaneous, and prepared to act on short notice, you can save a bundle on airfares.

American Net SAAver .... (800) 344-6702
http://www.americanair.com/aa_home/aans.html

Continental CO.O.L. .... (800) 231-0856
http://www.flycontinental.com/cool/

Northwest CyberSaverSM Fares .... (800) 692-6961
http://www.nwa.com/travel/cyber/cyber.html

TWA Trans World Specials.................................. (800) 872-8364
http://www.twa.com/odpairs

USAirways E-Savers .... (888) FLY-E-SAVERS
http://www.usair.com/travel/fares/esavers.htm

Here are some additional tips on air travel:

- Don't rely on the airlines' 800 numbers for the lowest fares — you can usually find lower fares. I have listed the airline phone numbers at the end of this chapter for making reservations, where can you ask them to match a price, and for those who have no access to the net.
- Advertised specials may not be the cheapest. Ask if an airline will match a fare you saw—it may be necessary to speak to a supervisor.
- Check into the discount airlines such as Southwest, Vanguard, or ATA; they often offer the lowest fare to the cities they fly to.
- Ask if there is a discount for children. Most domestic airlines don't offer this, but some, like American Airlines, offers a 50% discount for children under age 2. Most international flights offer a discount for all age children.

Only For The Truly Adventurous

There are some even more unusual ways to save money on travel, but these change the conventional ideas of what vacations mean. Most of us imagine a vacation to be on a plane or in a car or motel. There are some who travel by boat, but usually a cruise ship. To be different and save 1/2 off cruise ship rates, you could travel by sea freighter. These offer you a cabin room built for an officer (equivalent to a stateroom on a cruise ship) and three meals per day — just without the entertainment and endless food buffets. To investigate these options, call:

FREIGHTER WORLD CRUISES ....(626) 449-3106
http://freighterworld.com

MARIS ....(800) 99-MARIS
http://cruisemaris.com/freighters.html

If what you do during the vacation is boring to you, consider a vacation where you are a volunteer. There are several organizations that cater to the traveler who would like to put their time to good use. There is a book out called *Volunteer Vacations* (Chicago Review Press) that describes these types of vacations in detail and lists organizations throughout the world.

Dating Your Spouse

Lots of married couples also have both regular times set aside for dates and spur-of-the-moment get-aways as part of their regular life together. These "mini-mini-vacations" can be a source of real enjoyment and a needed break from busy routines at home and office.

It's not necessary to spend a lot of money on these dates—indeed, many can be done free. Before movie theaters, snow mobiles, ski lifts, or even cars, people had fun.

My husband and I need some time alone (as do most couples). We like to go on dates, but can't usually afford the combined cost of a sitter, dinner at a restaurant or movie theater tickets. So, we've found some cheaper alternatives that are as fun. Some people complain that these aren't as exciting as a dinner out or a movie. That may be true, but focus on why you're going out in the first place—to be together. Below are some of our ideas that we have tried. To find your own, think like a tourist: read the Sunday newspaper's travel section and get ideas, or read the visitor's guide published by your city.

Inexpen$ive Date Ideas

- *go on a walk at sunset time — it's beautiful and relaxing*
- *pick a handful of wildflowers for your partner*
- *go for a bike ride*
- *drive to the tallest place in the city and enjoy the view*
- *visit a factory or winery that offers free tours*
- *visit crafters in their studios (pottery, glass blowers, etc.)*
- *ride the public transit of your city, and see the town*
- *drive around the outer limits of the town*
- *read a play out loud to each other*
- *go rummage through a flea market*
- *visit a local art gallery*
- *go to a local bookstore's readings of poetry, or just browse*
- *go star gazing — many colleges have free observatory nights*
- *take a picnic basket to a park (do it indoors if it is rainy)*
- *go out for coffee and dessert instead of dinner*
- *go to matinees vs. nighttime shows—they are sometimes half price*
- *some employers sell theater tickets at half price*
- *go miniature golfing*
- *use two-for-one coupons for restaurants*
- *when it's too cold to walk outdoors, walk in a mall*
- *have a hot dog roast*
- *go square dancing*
- *have a taffy pull*
- *take advantage of the museums and any free days they may offer*
- *attend free music concerts in your city during summer and fall*
- *some bookstores offer free entertainment, especially on weekends*
- *send the kids to someone's house for the night*
- *enjoy the silence*

Helpful Travel Numbers and Websites

American Automobile Association (AAA) 800-482-5300
American Bed & Breakfast Association 804-379-2222
American Express 800-843-2273
American Youth Hostels 202-783-6161
Association of Elder Hostels 617-426-8056
Amtrak 800-387-1144
Caravan Trips for RV's 800-732-8337
Central Hotel Reservation Center 800-554-2220
(matches your budget to a hotel anywhere)
Condo Network 800-874-1411
Convention & Visitors Association 202-737-8866
KOA cabins 406-248-7444
Lodging Discounts..800-521-9640
Mississippi River Cruises 800-331-1467
National Park Service 202-208-4747
Steamboat Paddle Wheel Vacations......................800-543-1949
Steam Train Rides and Museums 800-356-0246
Travel Coupons (Entertainment Books) 313-637-8400
US Chamber of Commerce.....................................202-659-6000
Windjammer Sailing Cruises 800-327-2601
Western Union...800-325-6000

HTTP://WWW.TRAVELER.NET
Offers news clips, and links to other travel sites

HTTP://WWW.TRAVELOCITY.COM
Offers information on flights

HTTP://CITY.NET/FORMS/RESERVATIONS
Offers airfare price quotes and reservations

HTTP://WWW.FROMMERS.COM
Offers an encyclopedia of info on travel

Airline Phone Numbers

Aer Lingus	800-223-6537
Aero California	800-237-6225
Aeroflot	800-434-2300
Aerolineas Argentinas	800-333-0276
Air Aruba	800-882-7822
Air Canada	800-776-3000
Air China	800-986-1985
Air France	800-237-2747
Air Jamaica	800-523-5585
Air New Zealand	800-262-1234
Air South	800-247-7688
Alaska Airlines	800-426-0333
Alitalia Airlines	800-223-5730
All Nippon Airways	800-235-9262
Alm-Antillean	800-327-7230
Aloha Airlines	800-367-5250
America West	800-235-9292
American Airlines	800-433-7300
American Eagle	800-433-7300
American TransAir	800-225-2995
Asiana Airlines	800-227-4262
British Airlines	800-247-9297
Canadian Airlines	800-426-7000
Carnival Airlines	800-824-7386
Cathay Pacific	800-233-2742
Cayman Airlines	800-422-9626
China Airlines	800-227-5118
Continental	800-525-0280
Delta Airlines	800-221-1212
Egypt Air	800-334-6787
Eva Airlines	800-695-1188
Finnair	800-950-5000
Frontier Airlines	800-432-1359
Great Lakes Aviation	800-274-0662

HAWAIIAN AIRLINES 800-367-5320
HORIZON AIR 800-547-9308
IBERIA AIRLINES..800-772-4642
JAPAN AIRLINES...800-525-3663
KIWI INTERNATIONAL..................................800-538-5494
KLM ROYAL DUTCH.....................................800-374-7747
KOREAN AIR 800-438-5000
LONE STAR AIRLINES...................................800-877-3932
LITHUANIAN AIRLINES.................................800-711-3958
LUFTHANSA 800-645-3880
MALAYSIAN AIRLINES..................................800-421-8641
MESA AIRLINES 800-637-2247
MEXICANA AIRLINES 800-531-7921
MIDWEST EXPRESS......................................800-452-2022
NORTHWEST AIRLINES.................................800-225-2525
OLYMPIC AIRWAYS 800-223-1226
PHILIPPINE AIRLINES..................................800-435-9725
QANTAS AIRLINES..800-227-4500
RENO AIR 800-736-6247
SCANDINAVIAN AIRLINES............................800-221-2350
SINGAPORE AIRLINES..................................800-742-3333
SOUTH AFRICAN AIRLINES 800-722-9675
SWISSAIR...800-221-4750
TACA AIRLINES...800-535-8780
THAI AIRWAYS 800-426-5204
TOWER AIR...800-221-2500
TRISTAR AIRLINES.......................................800-218-8777
TWA 800-221-2000
UNITED AIRLINES..800-241-6522
UNITED EXPRESS 800-241-6522
USAIR..800-428-4322
VARIG 800-468-2744
VIRGIN ATLANTIC..800-862-8621

CHAPTER FIVE

Money, Money

Now is no time to think of what you do not have, think of what you can do with what there is.

–Ernest Hemingway, 1899-1961

Bankruptcies are near a record high. Consumer credit counseling is a booming business. Debt has become an acceptable form of supporting a desired lifestyle. Some people have taken control of their finances by digging out of debt, budgeting and actually saving some money. These people had to make a conscious decision in order to make this work. For some it took a wake-up call.

Getting a call from a collection agency or being turned down for a loan can provide that needed shock. Sometimes it takes the anger of a loved one to help us stop and see the deep water we have shopped our way into. Some of us ignore the call and keep living beyond our means. Others see they are out of control and get help.

Help can come in many forms. Credit counseling, budgeting, debt consolidation, and refinancing a mortgage are some of the tools used. Some are more profitable and reliable than others. Let's explore each of these tools, and see their helpfulness and pitfalls.

DEBT

Achieving a no-debt lifestyle is a rewarding feeling. The hard work it takes to get there is worth the blessings. Without debt, you are free: free to stay home, or make plans for a future event, go back to school, change careers or expand your family. Debt can sap the life out of us, causing us to worry and fret over bills. It instigates more fights between spouses than any other topic. It leads to much loss of personal property. It is something to be avoided and to make a serious effort to rid yourself of.

Debt Statistics

- *60% of American households carry some debt*
- *17% of the average household income is spent on debt*[11]
- *The combined personal debt in America is $1 trillion dollars*
- *Personal income is up 5% in America, but personal debt is up 13%*

Making more money doesn't usually solve the dilemma. Statistics show that the more we make, the higher our debt goes. Let's look at the facts:

- *50% of households earning $15,000 or less carry consumer debt*
- *60% of households earning up to $45,000 carry consumer debt*
- *70% of households earning $50,000 or more carry consumer debt*
- *in the past year, consumer debt has risen more than at any time in US history*
- *the average consumer is carrying $22,500 in debt (this does not include mortgages)*[12]

Financial analysts speculate that the debt has risen because we are hopeful for the future's economy, and are spending today, planning on paying it off in the future. This attitude can lead to our financial undoing. We can't bank on what tomorrow will bring. These same analysts have calculated that it would take an average annual income of $200,000 for a household to pay off the debt they are currently accumulating.[13]

This same "spend now/pay later" attitude reveals something about ourselves as well. It suggests that we are not accepting the limits of our income —we are living beyond our means. It suggests that we feel that we deserve more than we can afford.

In the first month of our marriage, Beau and I decided that we had a debt problem (a common newlywed realization). The carefree spending of our single years now was a large mess. We agreed that we had to plan a budget that included paying down those debts. To start our new financial lifestyle, we had a credit card cutting ceremony. We have a picture of this ceremony in our scrapbook, with Beau sitting in the middle of a pile of cut-up credit cards. We kept one general credit card (for emergencies), and a few gas cards.

Not everyone needs to cut up their cards. Some have more will power than others. If you lack the willpower, but want to have a card for emergencies, leave the card at home. A true emergency can wait for you to go home and get the card.

BUDGETING

One of the first steps to realizing financial control is to make a budget. A budget is a plan of attack. And no war can be won without a plan. There are many budget planning books on the market, and deciding where to start can be confusing. See the list of budgeting books we recommend in the back of this book.

Assessing the Damage

Most financial counselors suggest some basic steps to begin a debt reduction plan. First, they recommend that we assess the damage. We need to look at all of our obligations and spending habits before we can make a budget and plan our spending.

To get started with our obligations, it is recommended that we do the following:

1. List expenses for each month. Include:

federal taxes
state taxes
social security taxes
mortgage/rent
household expenses
homeowner's insurance (calculate monthly cost if annual)
property taxes or homeowner association fees
medical/dental insurance (calculate monthly cost if annual)
life insurance (calculate monthly cost if annual)

auto insurance (calculate monthly cost if annual)
auto payments
child support
day care
education costs
debts (list each individually: credit cards, loans)
utilities
food
entertainment (include cable TV)
magazine and newspaper subscriptions
book or video clubs
clothing store charge accounts
doctor/dentist bills
past due taxes
birthdays and holiday gifts
savings
hair care
allowances

If you do not know what you spend for some of the variable categories, such as food, examine several months of checkbook entries and receipts for an accurate total. Being honest about what you spend is very important at this point.

2. List all income for the month. Include:
salary
rent income
interest
dividends
child support
other

3. Compare your income to your expenses.
If you have more income than expenses, you are blessed. Use that blessing constructively. Save for a child's college fund, start a helping fund for less fortunate friends and their emergencies, or invest for your retirement.

If your expenses exceed your income, here are a few things to look at before you start panicking:

- *Are you keeping accurate records?*
- *Do you balance the checkbook often?*

- *Have you spent money on unplanned impulse items?*
- *Have you planned for birthday and holiday gifts?*

Gifts can break a budget. There are several ways to tackle this obstacle:

- *make gifts or crafts instead of buying something*
- *draw names at holidays so there are fewer people to buy for*
- *don't use credit cards for gifts*
- *send cards instead of gifts*
- *buy throughout the year at thrift shops and sales so you are stocked when a need arises*
- *calculate how many gifts you buy each year*

To help plan for the many gifts that you may need to buy, consider creating a gift planner. List all of the possible gifts you may encounter, estimate how much to spend on each, total the sum and divide by 12. This is the amount you need to save each month to cover gifts. Here is a list of gifts you may need to plan for:

birthdays	Father's Day	graduations
anniversaries	Valentine's Day	weddings
Christmas	Easter	baby showers
Mother's Day	bridal showers	

Ways to Avoid Impulse Shopping

- *Use lay-away purchasing. It requires you to have the money before you buy something. It also helps you think about whether you really need that item.*
- *Wait 30 days before you decide to buy anything.*
- *Have a rule that you and your spouse cannot buy anything over $5 without discussing it first.*

Making A Budget

Now that you know what you spend and earn, put yourself on a money diet. Deciding where to trim and what to keep can be confusing. What should your clothing allotments be? How much should we spend on food? What is a reasonable entertainment amount?

Every financial counselor will have their own answers to these questions. What is reasonable may also vary depending on what part of the country you live in. For example, in the San Francisco Bay Area, it is common for people to spend 50% of their income on mortgage payments or rent, whereas in the Midwest 25% is more common. Below are some general guidelines that were written to appeal to everyone.

Suggested Budget Percentages (after taxes and tithe)

Housing (rent, utilities, household needs)	*38%*
Food	*12%*
Cars (payments, maintenance)	*15%*
Debts	*5%*
Insurance (life and homeowner)	*5%*
Entertainment (include cable TV)	*5%*
Clothing	*5%*
Medical/dental (bills & insurance)	*5%*
Savings	*5%*
Miscellaneous	*5%*

Taken from A Guide To Family Budgeting, *Larry Burkett, 1993, p. 13-25.*

Since every household has varying needs, adjust these percentages as needed. Some may need to add daycare, while others have higher medical needs. Others may know that their car will probably die in a few years, so they should save now for another one. Adjust the numbers to fit your needs, taking from some areas and adding where needed.

Here is a sample budget for a household income of $35,000 (which is the current average income for a household in the United States), using the recommended percentages from the above chart. These figures may not coincide with incomes, expenses, and deductions in your living area.

Income	*2,916*
Expenses	
taxes (28%)	*816*
tithe	*290*

Household	*660*
mortgage/rent	
household expenses	
property taxes or association fees	
utilities	
telephone	
maintenance	
Insurance	*90*
homeowner's	
life	
Medical	*90*
medical/dental insurance	
doctor/dentist bills	
Automobile	*270*
insurance	
payments	
maintenance	
gasoline	
Debts (list each individually)	*90*
departments stores	
VISA or MasterCard	
clothing store charge accounts	
past due taxes	
child support	
Clothing	*90*
Food	*250*
Entertainment	*90*
cable TV	
magazine subscriptions	
book or video clubs	
vacations	
Savings	*90*
Miscellaneous	*90*
allowances	
haircuts	
dry cleaning	
gifts	
cash for spending	

Free Budget Planners

Consumer Alert, a 20-year old national consumer group, offers a free two page budget planner. It contains a budget worksheet and suggestions on starting a budget. To get this, send a self-addressed stamped envelope to:

CONSUMER ALERT
Budget Planner Offer
1001 Connecticut Ave NW
Suite 1128
Washington D.C. 20036

Sticking To A Budget

Making a budget is much easier than sticking to one. It is much like a food diet: we plan and intend to stick to the diet, but we keep on eating those brownies because they taste so good. Spending is fun. The daily temptation to buy things is strong. Seeing advertisements on television constantly tell us that we aren't complete without this or that. Or that we are "missing out" or "less cool" than everyone else if we don't modernize and consume. We get tired of saying "no" and we spend. A more dangerous tendency is to have the attitude that "we deserve this."

To stay motivated with your budget, try these tricks:

- *remember the reason you are budgeting in the first place; think about the debt you have or the plans you are trying to make*
- *go to the bank once per week and withdraw what the budget allots for that week; do not return to the bank or ATM until the next week—only spend what you have*
- *if you have any leftover money at the end of each week, put it in a bank or special envelope and save for a special occasion, purchase or to help someone in need*
- *don't go to the mall unless you have a specific reason—only one in four people in the malls are there for a particular purchase, and 93% of American girls say store hopping is their favorite activity*[14]

Finding Hidden Money

When I quit my job, we lost 50% of our income. We didn't move or sell a car. When we looked at our budget and the deficit we had, we found extra money for some bills by redoing our food budget. We cut our groceries by

60% and used that extra money for other expenses. The specific steps on how we did it are in my first book, *Miserly Moms—Living On One Income In A Two Income Economy.*

Ways To Reduce Debt

Sometimes our debt exceeds our income considerably and any attempts at stretching the budget can't cover the deficit. Before considering a second income, look at some of the alternatives to reducing debt. Here are some of the tools people use:

Debt Pay Down Plan

In a debt pay down plan, you are giving each creditor a payment each month. Plan on paying off the loan with the lowest balance first. When that bill is paid off, take the amount applied to that monthly bill and add it to the amount being paid to the bill with the next lowest balance. Each time you pay one off, roll over that amount to the next one. This has a snowball effect, adding momentum to the next bill, and so on, until they are all gone!

Here is a sample of a debt pay down plan:

Bill	*Balance*	*Payment Months*						
		1	*2*	*3*	*4*	*5*	*6*	*7*
A	*$75*	*25*	*25*	*25*				
B	*$600*	*50*	*50*	*50*	*75*			
C	*$1500*	*100*	*100*	*100*	*100*	*175*		

Notice that the monthly payments increase as the previous debt is paid off.

Other Tips:

Try and surpass the minimum due if you can. Paying a little extra adds up. For example, if you had a loan balance of $3000 and you paid the minimum each month, it would take you approximately 30 years to pay it off, and you would end up paying $10,000. If, however, you paid an extra $5 to the minimum payment, you would pay off the balance in half the time and with half the total amount paid.

Another tip is to find a credit card with a lower annual percentage rate (APR) than the one you are paying. If so, transfer your amounts to that card, but do not spend more. Close the other account. This just reduces the amount of finance charge you will be paying as you pay down the debt. Don't be fooled by the low introductory rates that inflate in a few months. Choose one that remains low until you can pay it off. Don't keep transferring the balance from account to account instead of paying the debt.

If you have a savings account, many financial counselors recommend using it to pay down the debt. The reason is that savings accounts earn much less interest than that being charged by your credit cards. You may also consider selling some assets to pay off the debt (jewelry, extra real estate, second car, antiques, newer car for an older one).

Ask a lender if they will offer you a discount on the interest rate if you make payments automatically from your checking account.

Don't make late payments on any account. The finance charges will wipe out any progress that you made on paying down the balance.

Debtors Support Group

There is a support group for debtors, fashioned after the 12 step program of Alcoholics Anonymous. It's called Debtors Anonymous. They have weekly meetings to cope with debt problems.

For a contact in your area, contact:

Debtors Anonymous
P.O. Box 20322
New York, NY 10025
(212) 642-8222

Refinance Your Mortgage

By refinancing your mortgage, you take out a loan that will cover your mortgage as well as all of your debts. This reduces your overall payments, but extends the amount of your debt for 30 years. You also lose all equity you have built up and are starting all over each time you refinance. I know people who do this regularly so that they can continue to live beyond their means. When they retire, they will have a surprise with large monthly payments to make throughout their golden years.

If you decide to go this route, keep a few things in mind:

- *don't use this option often; your debt is still there, just masked in another payment*
- *don't use the lower payments as an excuse to spend more*
- *it isn't cost effective unless: 1) you can get a rate 1% lower than your current mortgage, and 2) you plan on staying in the house for at least 2 years (this covers closing costs)*

Credit Counseling

Credit counselors act as a liaison between you and the creditors. They may get the creditors to agree on lower monthly payments, or to not make collection proceedings. Creditors tend to respond to credit counselors because they believe the debtor is serious about repaying if they have hired one, and they have come to know and trust credit counselors. Credit counselors will take your bills and your income to cover them, and be in control of both each month. You will be given an allowance to use for your other expenses.

There are some pitfalls to credit counseling that should be considered before going this route:

- *credit counseling tends to go unregulated in many states, leaving people at the mercy of con artists who are really salesmen of high interest credit cards*
- *check to see if the credit counselor is certified by the National Certification Board of the National Foundation For Consumer Credit (800) 388-2227*
- *the credit counseling fee should be no more than $10-25 per month, since they are usually funded by banks or other organizations*

To find a credit counselor in your area, call the Consumer Credit Counseling Service (CCCS) for an office nearest you (see number below).

Helpful Numbers

Consumer Credit Counseling Service ....(800) 388-CCCS
A national non-profit organization that offers free and low-cost credit counseling and education

National Center For Financial Education.........(619) 232-8811
Offers free booklets on debt reduction

Debt Consolidation

Debt consolidation is when a loan is taken out to cover all of the debts. Your monthly payment will be lower than the combined bills. Not everyone considers this option to be very helpful for the following reasons:

- *there are fees for these loans that average 10% of the loan amount (more debt!)*
- *the interest rates on these loans may be higher than your credit card is currently charging*
- *you are replacing an unsecured credit card debt with a loan against your home; a credit card company has little recourse in collecting their debt, whereas defaulting on a loan with a home as collateral can lead to the loss of your home*
- *the loan may hinder your ability to sell your home or refinance a mortgage since the loan's value may exceed your equity*
- *the interest on these loans may not be deductible*
- *with a debt pay down plan or CCCS intervention you may have paid off your debts in a few years; but with the loan, you have spread the same debts over 30 years*
- *be careful that the agent selling you the loan isn't an attorney that also may later attempt to convince you to use his services in bankruptcy court*

Identity Theft

Some people have gotten into financial hot water without realizing it. Some people have had their identity stolen by someone, and debt incurred under their name. If this has happened to you, write a notarized letter to the creditor stating that it is not your doing.

To prevent it from happening, take these precautions:

- *tear up those preapproved credit card offers; thieves can use them to open an account*
- *get your name removed from the credit-bureau mailing lists: Equifax 888-567-8688, Experian (formerly TRW) 800-353-0809, Trans Union 800-680-7293*
- *NEVER give any personal information to a telephone solicitor*

- *don't write (or let someone else write) credit card numbers on a check; your check gets seen by hundreds of processors before going to the bank*
- *don't give your social security number to anyone unless you know them and understand their need to have it*
- *check your credit report annually*

Some credit reporting agencies charge a fee of $8-$10, but in certain states it is free. Many credit reporting agencies will give each person a free report each year. Equifax 800-685-1111, Experian 888-397-3742, Trans Union 800-888-4213. Check for:

- *accounts that are not yours*
- *accounts that you closed but show active*
- *past due accounts*
- *unpaid balances you thought were paid*

Bankruptcy

This is not an option that I would encourage, since I believe that we need to be responsible for ourselves and our actions. However, many feel they are cornered. According to the National Bankruptcy Review Commission, more than a million households file for bankruptcy each year. And the number rises each year. Most causes for the bankruptcy were listed as medical debt from uninsured people, and credit card debt.

Bankruptcy is often referred to as filing Chapter 7, 11 or 13. Let's look at each type.

Chapter 7 is a liquidation of all assets and distribution of the money to the creditors. All debts are discharged, whether or not there was enough money to cover the debts. Occasionally a portion of the home equity is spared, but a lawyer can explain your situation best. This action gives the debtor a fresh start. This works for most debts, but does not cover debts for:

- *child support or alimony*
- *taxes owed for the past 3 years (older than 3 years are covered)*
- *student loans*
- *money owed for intentional and willful misconduct*
- *secured debts (like home loans)*

Chapter 11 is a reorganization of finances usually used by businesses, but can be used by individuals. Chapter 11 allows the debtor to remain in control of all possessions and businesses, and continue to manage the estate, all while working with the creditors. This is very expensive with filing fees and lawyers and can take several months to settle. The goal of Chapter 11 is to settle on a repayment plan with your creditors. This can usually be achieved with less money and take less time by filing Chapter 13.

Chapter 13 is another form of reorganization. It repays all debts in full, but allows you more time to do it. By filing Chapter 13, you can have up to 60 months to repay existing debts. You are given a trustee whom you give one amount for all of the debts each month and they distribute the payments. In order to file for Chapter 13, you must have a steady income, and your unsecured debts (credit cards) must not exceed $250,000.

Since any of these are a serious step, and laws vary in states, consult an attorney before making this decision. Keep in mind that a debtor who files bankruptcy has damaged his credit rating for up to ten years. This is in addition to the emotional turmoil created for you. For more information on bankruptcy, contact the Bureau of Consumer Protection-Office of Consumer & Business Education at (202) 326-3650.

You Don't Have To Take It

If you are being harassed by a bill collection agency, you can stop those phone calls and letters. Under the Fair Debt Collection Practices Act, collectors must stop calling and writing if you send them a letter requesting this. Half of the states in the US also require this same practice of the original loan issuer. If they do not comply, contact the Federal Trade Commission, Washington D.C. 20580.

SAVING

Many Americans do not have a savings account. For those who do save, the amount saved is a much smaller percentage of their income than in most other progressive nations. This lack of saving usually leaves us lacking when an emergency hits. And we turn to borrowing money in order to survive.

Starting the saving habit is easy. We need to start putting money aside each month, no matter how small. If we start small it is easier to ease into this. And if that money is used wisely, it could grow and provide you with a cushion.

A financial newsletter did a comparison of what two people would have after 40 years of saving $50 per month. One person only saved $50 per month for 8 years, but let it sit and compound after that until she was age 65. Her total contribution was $4800, but at age 65 she had $256,650. The other didn't add any money to his account for the first 8 years, then added $50 per month for the next 35 years. His total contribution was $22,200, but after 35 years he only had $217,830. The moral of the story is, save as soon as you can. It adds up.

Ways To Save

Once you have decided that some sort of savings is a good idea, putting that money away can be tricky. It's tempting to do something else with it. So try these steps to help save:

- *start with a payroll deduction so that you never see the money*
- *when you are done paying a loan, take that monthly amount and put it in the savings account*
- *invest the savings into a high earning account (stocks, mutual funds, CDs, savings bonds); see section below for details on investing*
- *take advantage of an employer's 401K and any matching fund programs*
- *take your spare change at the end of each day and put it in a jar; at the end of each month invest it in a mutual fund or stock*
- *stop smoking and put the extra cash in savings*
- *take a sack lunch more often and put the savings in the bank (this savings can range from $60-100 per month)*
- *instead of buying that lottery ticket, put that dollar in the bank (your return will be better)*
- *instead of eating out, put that $25 you would spend in a savings account*

INVESTING

By investing your money instead of having it sit in a savings account, you may double your money in half the time that it would take in a traditional savings account. You don't have to have much money in order to invest. Nor do you need to be on the phone three times per day to a stock broker, or follow the New York Stock exchange's daily fluctuations to make some money with investments.

Here are some tips for investing your saved money:

- *research the type of investment you are considering (stocks, bonds, real estate) for the pitfalls and strengths*
- *go for high yield investing*
- *don't put all of your savings in one type of investment — spread it out between stocks, mutual funds, real estate, etc.*
- *many mutual funds will waive the large initial investment requirement of $500-$1000 if you agree to a monthly investment amount of $50 or more (there may be a few who will accept payments of $25 per month)*
- *only buy no-load mutual funds (a load is a fee to sign up)*
- *don't invest in a mutual fund that focuses on only one market area (i.e. scientific research, Asian markets, gold, etc.); invest in broader spectrum mutual funds*
- *look for a rate that, after you pay taxes on the interest, has a return of at least 3% (i.e. 7% CD rate, after taxes realizes 5.5%)*
- *invest the money in a retirement account; you receive a tax deduction for the deposit, and you save for the future*
- *use a low cost broker; they often charge 70% less than full service brokers. Some reputable ones are:*

  CHARLES SCHWAB 800-435-4000
  FIDELITY BROKERAGE 800-544-7272
  QUICK & REILLY 800-221-5220

- *buy low and sell high*
- *check out the company—get information from the broker*
- *real estate is usually a good investment, rising slowly in value in some areas, and in other areas rising quicker; select property carefully since some do not rise in value, and some even fall in value; make sure that you can cover your costs with the rental income (property management, taxes, mortgage, non-rental periods)*
- *save for college using US Savings Bonds; these defer interest taxation to when used, then only taxed on parents income, and only if above a certain level if purchased in parent's name*

- *if you buy in the student's name and cash it in after they turn 14, they are taxed at the child rate*
- *buy US Bonds—they are guaranteed by the Federal Government, rates adjust every 6 months to meet inflation, and they are exempt from state and local taxes (to benefit from these, you need a long term investment)*

CHAPTER SIX

Insurance

Don't go to a doctor whose plants have died.

—Erma Bombeck

HOMEOWNERS INSURANCE

Whether you are a renter or a homeowner, you should have protection for your home and your goods. The loss of your goods or home is devastating. There are so many ways that our homes can be damaged. We should try to get a policy that covers them all—inexpensively. We also need to be careful that we are covered for what we think we are paying for.

Aside from protecting the building and contents, a homeowner or renter's policy provides other coverage you may be surprised about. For the extras, see the section below "Coverage You Didn't Know You Had."

Making sure you are covered properly is important. Make sure that you have coverage for the areas listed below.

The Dwelling

This is the building that you live in, with any attached buildings, such as a garage. You mainly should be worried about the cost of rebuilding your home. To find out exactly what you need, find out what the average cost is to build in your area (per square foot). This can be found by contacting a local builder's association. Multiply this figure by the square feet in your home and insure for that amount.

Make sure that you have replacement value coverage. This means that as the cost of rebuilding rises over time, your policy will still cover the full cost of the damage. Without this coverage, the insurance company could say that you will only get a percentage of the value.

If you live in a townhouse or condominium, ask the homeowner's association to clarify what part of the building structure is your responsibility. Also check if any of the grounds are your responsibility. Some yards are the responsibility of the association while others are the responsibility of the homeowner.

Any Other Structures On Your Property

This would cover anything other than the home and garage. A wood shop or greenhouse would come under this category.

Loss Of Use Of Your Building

This provides coverage for expenses you incur while the building is unlivable. These expenses may be the motel you need to live in for a few weeks while repairs are done, or the meals you need to buy at a restaurant while the kitchen is rebuilt after a grease fire.

Check if you have protection for things you may have that are out of the ordinary. Some things to check for are:

Home Office

If you have an office at home, most policies only cover $2500 of damage to the equipment. Since most computers and other gadgets kept in the home office amount to more than that, you may want to purchase extra coverage.

Earthquake Policy

Having grown up in earthquake country and having lived through some real shakers, I advise anyone living near a fault line to purchase earthquake coverage. It is an extra financial burden, but well worth it when everything literally comes crashing in on you.

After the big earthquake in 1989, we saw so many homeowners who had no home left but had to continue paying the mortgage they had. Then they had to pay for the new loan to rebuild the home. Many foreclosed or sold at a loss. An earthquake policy would have prevented that loss.

Flood Insurance

A shocking 90% of flood victims are not covered for their damage. Most general policies do not carry flood insurance. It is an extra coverage that has a surcharge. If you live anywhere near a flood zone, make sure you get the coverage you need. If you cannot get flood coverage (many insurance providers won't offer it), check into the federally administered insurance program offered by FEMA (National Flood Insurance, FEMA/MSC, P.O. Box 1038, Jessup, MD 20797-9408 or call 888-CALL-FLOOD or check out http://www.fema.gov/fema/nfip96-46.shm). They will refer you to an agent in your area who will offer you flood insurance.

Personal Valuables

If you have special antiques or family jewelry that is valuable, make sure they are covered by your homeowner's policy. Many policies pay a very small amount in case of theft or loss, and it isn't usually enough to replace much.

Replacement Cost Insurance

Make sure that you are covered for what it will actually cost to replace the items in your home as well as your building. Insuring for market value is not recommended by consumer groups. That coverage usually is including your land and may not cover the rebuilding costs. Many policies cover a depreciated value, and not the cost of replacing it.

Old Buildings Coverage

This is not the actual name of the coverage type, but it gets the point across. If you have an older building that could have defects in it from age, a building inspector could order it demolished for safety reasons. The cost of this and rebuilding won't be fully covered by your regular policy. An extended coverage will take care of any gaps.

Odd Things to Check For

Some policies cover more extras than others. Some of these things may be important to you. You may need extra coverage for things. A few coverage items to check for are:

- *falling objects*
- *the weight of snow or ice causing damage*
- *water damage from appliances*
- *damage from any appliance*
- *freezing damage to pipes and water systems*
- *electrical malfunctions that cause damage*

Renter's Insurance

When renting a home you want to make sure your possessions in the home are adequately insured. The owner is only responsible for the structure and the grounds. You are responsible to insure your belongings inside the home. If you own a waterbed, make sure your insurance covers this. Sometimes that is an extra rider. Also, make sure you are covered for loss of use in case of calamity.

Mobile Home Insurance

A mobile home owner has both the headaches of a renter and a homeowner. They are renters since the land is not theirs and they pay rent to use the association property and amenities, but they are homeowners since they have the responsibility of the mobile home. Make sure you are covered for the loss of the mobile home itself if damaged, and loss of its use you suffer. Make sure you are covered for damage if the unit is moved.

Some lenders will feel better if you have a policy that protects them. Since the home can be moved, but it is also the collateral for the loan, you are a higher risk than a stationary home. This protects the leinholder if you skip town with the home.

Limits of Liability

Most policies limit what they will pay for certain categories.
Here are a few examples (your policy may have different limits):

- *Lost cash — $200*
- *Securities, bank notes, tickets, collectors stamps, etc. — $1000*
- *Jewelry -$1000*
- *Firearms -$2000*

- *Silverware- $2500*
- *Office equipment — $2500*
- *Personal property at another location — $250*

Not Covered

Some things will not be covered under any policy. Sometimes a rider can be purchased separately for some of these. Here is a sample of common exclusions:

- *sink holes*
- *freeze damage to a vacant dwelling*
- *vandalism to a vacant dwelling*
- *repeated water damage by an appliance*
- *water damage from floods, backed up sewers, leaking swimming pools, underground streams.*
- *power failures (that are area wide)*
- *neglect*
- *earth movement (quakes or slides)*
- *war*
- *nuclear incident*
- *decisions made by local government*
- *pets*
- *motor vehicles damaged in a fire or calamity of the home*
- *water crafts, snow mobiles, all terrain vehicles, jet skis, hang gliders*
- *property of tenants*
- *bookkeeping material*
- *intentional acts by you*
- *damages caused by business activity on the property*
- *defective or decaying material*
- *damages caused by a vehicle to the building*

How to Keep the Cost Down

Shop Around

Premiums are not the same at every company, even though they cover the same locations. Rates can have a range of $200 per year.

Keep a High Deductible

The minimum deductible is usually $250 on a homeowner's policy. By raising that to $500 or $1000, you can deduct up to 25% off your annual premiums. Remember that insurance is to help pay for things our savings cannot cover.

Don't Over or Under Insure

Get a policy that covers your needs only. Don't try and get rich off of your calamities by having inflated coverage.

Replace Your Dwelling Only

Many people insure their home for market value. This is coverage of the home plus the property. You only need to get coverage for the building structure and contents, not the land.

Investigate Discounts

You can save money on policies in a number of areas. Ask your agent if you get discounts for fire detectors, alarm systems, dead bolts, fire extinguishers, multi-policies (having auto and home with the same carrier), nonsmoker household, long term customer, mature residents with no children, retirees, and fire resistant roofing material. These are just a few areas to ask about. Some of these discounts can offer as much as a 15% discount on the premium.

Don't Skip Around

Jumping from carrier to carrier will eventually catch up with you. Staying with one carrier will offer you a history with them that may lead to a discount.

Coverage You Didn't Know You Had

Many people have some extra coverage provided by their homeowner's policy that they may not know about. Here are a few examples:

- *debris removal caused by a natural disaster, such as a fallen tree or collapsed wall from high wind*
- *trees or shrubs lost to natural causes (high winds, freezing, etc.)*
- *if you live in a rural area and have to pay for fire protection services*
- *check forgery or credit card fraud up to a certain limit*
- *loss of your luggage or wallet*
- *if your child throws a ball and breaks a neighbor's window, your insurance will probably pay for it*
- *some policies even pay for legal fees (but not damages) if you are sued for slander, false arrest, wrongful eviction, or invasion of privacy*
- *damaged carpeting from spilled bleach is sometimes covered*

Many of these you may want to pay for yourself. You need to weigh the cost of the damage over the possibility of being categorized as a high risk customer, and thus pay higher premiums in the future.

CAR INSURANCE

Car insurance is a topic filled with anger and frustration. It is required to legally drive, but many feel it is filled with excessive fees and pricing mysteries. Sometimes we are buying coverage we do not need, and other times we are driving on thin ice.

What We Pay For:

Understanding what our policy prices are based on sometimes help us know how to shop better for coverage. Here are some variables that affect insurance prices:

Location

Where you live determines how much the rate will be. Your state, city and neighborhood determine the base rate that you will pay. They figure that most accidents occur within a few miles of our homes, so they figure your likelihood to have an accident based on where you live.

Age

Your age tells the insurance companies how mature you might be, and therefore how responsible you should be. Drivers under 25 and above 65 pay a higher rate than other ages.

Gender

Young single men are statistically worse drivers and will pay a higher rate than a woman of the same age.

Marital Status

A married person tends to be more responsible and will have lower rates than a single person of that age. You might be able to keep your married person's discount after a divorce if you have custody of one or more children. It's worth asking.

Use Of The Car
How much you drive the car will affect the rates you pay. The rates for a pleasure car will be less than a car used for business or for commuting to work. The number of miles you drive each year determines the rate as well.

Type Of Car
The type of car you drive also determines the insurance premium you pay. You will pay a higher premium for a 4 wheel drive or recreation vehicle than a minivan. Also, the cost of the car determines the rate. An expensive Mercedes-Benz will cost more to repair than a lesser expensive vehicle. If a vehicle is known for its safety features, it may cost less to drive. A car's ages and ease of obtaining repair parts will affect the rate.

Driving Record
Your personal driving record also will determine how much you pay. Each moving violation warns the insurance agency that you are a risky driver, and they will charge you for that extra risk. This can be seen as a generally higher rate, or as a surcharge that stays on the policy for several years.

How to Save on Auto Insurance

Deductibles
If you have a higher deductible, your monthly rates will go down. This means that you are willing to assume a greater share of the damages when they happen. Insurance companies like this.

Lower the Coverage
By changing to the minimum coverage allowed, you can reduce your premiums. Make sure you are covered sufficiently for an accident (medical, time off work, cars involved, etc.), but take no more than that.

Reduce Collision And Comprehensive
If you have a newer car, repairing a scratch or dent will be costly, and you need the comprehensive and collision coverage. If, however, your car is older (5-10 years old), repairing the same will cost less. Lowering your comprehensive coverage will save you in cases like this.

Omit The Extras
There are some coverage categories that are not required, and are a savings to avoid. The road side services coverage is not necessary if you are a mem-

ber of a travel club, like AAA. See if you can do without it. Some consumer groups do not, however, recommend dropping the uninsured motorist coverage or the liability coverage.

Shop Around

Not all agencies charge the same rates for the same neighborhood. One company considered my neighborhood a high rate area. Another thought it a good neighborhood and offered lower rates for the same coverage.

Driving Style

Improve your driving record and your rates will go down. It may take a few years to get rid of a violation, but staying alert and driving safe will bring it down.

Buy The Right Car

When buying a car, keep in mind the insurance you will have to pay on it. If you can, call your insurance company before you buy a car and ask which models and companies have the lower rates.

Look For Discounts

There are a number of discounts that will lower your premium. Some are:

- *Multi-car discount: having both cars insured with the same company will give you a discount on both cars.*
- *Other policies: if you have other policies (home, life, medical) with the same company, you will receive a discount on all of the policies.*
- *Non-smoking: by not smoking you may receive a discount.*
- *Anti-theft Devices: if you install anti-theft devices you will lower your rates.*
- *Air-Bags: some companies offer a discount if air-bags are installed.*
- *Good driver discount: if you have a clean driving record, you can get a discount on the car you drive.*
- *Good Student discount: if a younger driver (under age 25) is on your policy, his/her good grades may lower their premiums.*
- *Middle Age Discount: if you are between the ages of 50 and 65 you may be offered a lower rate.*
- *Low Mileage: if you drive a very little amount each year, you may get a discount.*

Coverage You May Not Know You Have

Did you know that there are ways to cover those blunders that you may not have thought of?

We found out about an unusual way to pay for some damage done to a relative's new car. We went to a wedding that had the reception at a polo club and field. The cars were parked on the polo field. The kids had a tree house to play in that overlooked the polo field. My son decided to see how far the polo ball could fly out of the tree house window, forgetting there were cars below. He put a nice dent in the hood of a brand new car. The damage was close to $300. Our auto insurance wouldn't cover it, but our homeowner policy did (less our deductible). The owner of the car suggested we look into the homeowner's policy. He knew about this from his own son's growing up years.

The same goes for items that are stolen out of or damaged accidentally by your car. These would be covered under the homeowner's policy. If you have an accident (such as tripping over the seatbelt as you get out of the car) that incurs medical expenses, these would be covered by the medical portion of your car insurance. If you rent a car and it gets stolen or wrecked, some automobile insurance covers you. Check with your agent before you waive the rental company's coverage.

LIFE INSURANCE

Life insurance is one of those necessary evils in life. It's something we'd probably rather not think about. It is there to provide for loved ones in order to protect their lifestyle after the breadwinner dies. Some people may not need much life insurance. Young people will most likely have no one to provide for, but may want a minimal policy to cover funeral expenses and outstanding debts. People without dependents or whose children are grown and independent, or those leaving no debts to their survivors could do without life insurance.

I know of several families who carry no insurance of any type. Most of these are barely able to provide for the family with what they bring home. This is a hard call to make, but hopefully they are considering the devastation that may follow their death if no insurance is bought. Some expect Social Security to take care of their needs. This may not be a good idea since at the time of this writing, the future stability of that institution is in question, and the amount that Social Security pays is barely enough to pay the rent. A few families somehow find the money for cable TV, toys for the kids, or theater tickets, but cannot seem to afford insurance. Most families can get a decent policy for less than $50 per month.

Types of Life Insurance

There are two main types of life insurance: term life and cash value. Below is a brief description of each and some pros and cons.

Term Life Insurance

A term policy provides the face value of the benefit, and no more. Premiums are lower in the younger years and increase as you age. This type of policy is recommended by consumer groups.

There are different types of term life insurance. Mortgage insurance is a type of term life insurance, called decreasing term life insurance. The premium remains the same, but its value is shrinking over time, as the mortgage balance shrinks.

PROS:

- *your premiums will be lower (up to 80% lower than cash value insurance) during your younger years for the same benefit amount as cash value insurance*
- *you are free to invest your other money elsewhere, where you can have better control and decision making power, and will probably get a greater rate of return*
- *you are paying less of a commission fee (up to a 20% savings)*

CONS:

- *your premiums will increase as you age*
- *coverage may terminate at the end of its term because some are not renewable; this could be a problem since obtaining insurance at an older age can be more difficult and expensive*

Cash Value Life Insurance

These types of policies accrue interest over the life of the policy. They can go under the name of annuity plans, endowment plans, variable life insurance, traditional whole life, single-premium whole life, interest-sensitive whole life and universal life insurance.

They cost more than term policies because they provide both a life insurance coverage as well as an investment. These are the type of policies that most insurance agents will recommend, however most consumer groups do not.

PROS:

- *the premiums will remain stable regardless of the increasing age of the insured*
- *if the policy is not used by retirement age, it can be used as income*
- *some policies can be guaranteed for life*
- *the IRS will not usually tax you on the earnings you are accruing*

CONS:

- *your premiums would be higher in the early years for the same benefit amount as a term insurance premium*
- *you cannot control the earnings on the investment amount*
- *you may earn more elsewhere with your investment because the insurance company must pay a financial manager with a portion of your proceeds*
- *some types of cash-value policies do not pay the beneficiary the investment portion of their policy*

Where to Buy

After you have decided what type of life insurance to buy, the next question is who to buy it from. There are close to 2000 companies that sell life insurance, all wanting your business. Some will provide better service, better financial stability, and some will provide a better return on your money.

To better understand your policy or your coverage needs, contact:

NATIONAL INSURANCE CONSUMER ORGANIZATION
121 Payne St.
Alexandria, VA 22314
800-942-4242 or 703-549-8050

They are a division of the Insurance Information Institute—800-331-9146.

To get a rating on a company, call A.N. Best at 908-439-2200. You are looking for an A or better rating.

To find out the financial strength of an insurance company, contact Weiss Research. They will prepare a verbal report for $15, a one page brief for $25, or an extensive 20 page report for $45. Or look on the Internet for Insurance News Network for a free peek at the company's financial strength *(http://www.insure.com)*.

There are many services that will offer you quotes on life insurance. Some carry more companies in their database than others. Most of these services are free to you since the insurance companies pay for the service. But not all companies want to pay this fee, so not all are listed when you call for a quote. If there are some companies you are interested in, call them yourself.

Free Quote Services

COMPANY	PHONE NUMBER	INTERNET ADDRESS	TOTAL COMPANIES LISTED
LifeRates	*800-457-2837*	*none*	*200*
MasterQuote	*800-337-LIFE*	*http://www.masterquote.com*	*200*
AccuQuote	*800-442-9899*	*http://www.accuquote.com*	*190*
Quotesmith	*800-431-1147*	*http://www.quotesmith.com*	*132*
TermQuote	*800-444-8376*	*http://www.rcinet.com/termquote/*	*10*
SelectQuote	*800-343-1985*	*http://www.selectquote.com*	*18*
InsuranceQuote	*800-972-1104*	*http://www.iquote.com*	*80*

When you call for a quote, many companies require lots of information. Be prepared to provide them with information like your cholesterol count, blood pressure, weight, height, etc.

Ways to Save

For the best savings, take advantage of any group policies that you may be eligible for. Compared to individual policies, you may save up to 50%.

Look for them in your workplace, clubs, spouse's clubs or service groups, universities, fraternities, unions, and any military organizations. Many employers offer 2 times the employee's annual salary as a free benefit, and then allow the purchase of subsequent coverage at a low fee. This will be your best deal.

To the insurance company we are a statistic: a group type, a risk category and an age bracket. These are what determine our costs for coverage. But not all companies consider the same statistic to be at the same level of risk. For example, one company may consider the area that you live as more risky than another company does. So, shop around.

Try to lower your premiums before you shop. One way you can is to stop smoking. That alone can save you a bundle.

Also look at mail order insurance providers. Their premiums will be lower because they have no insurance agent's commission to pay. This can save you as much as 20%.

Another way to save as much as 35% is to purchase a policy with your spouse. This type is called a first-to-die policy, and pays just like it sounds. This is cheaper than 2 individual policies.
Insuring a child is not recommended since life insurance is to provide for those left behind that depended on you for income.

When buying a policy, ask for any future rate guarantees they can provide, and if the policy is renewable.

Avoid special travel insurance like the ones sold in airports. These are usually covered by general life insurance policies and are not necessary.

And The Winner Is...

The lowest rates available usually go to someone who falls into all of these categories:

- *nonsmoker for the past four years*
- *"normal" blood pressure without medication*
- *no serious illnesses*
- *not overweight (according to their charts)*
- *low cholesterol*
- *no deaths in the immediate family from heart disease before age 60*

How Much to Buy

The key to providing for your family is to assess their needs, if a breadwinner dies. That could mean allowing for the survivor not to return to work for an extended period of time. Or perhaps the survivor does not currently work. Then, providing for current income for a period of time is important.

The "period of time" factor is something that needs to be decided upon by the family. How long do they want that current level of income? Some financial counselors recommend between 5-10 years worth of expenses.

Other factors to take into consideration are any outstanding debts that would be left to the family, any business loans, taxes that would be due on the sale of a business, medical bills, estate taxes, moving costs if applicable, college tuition for the children, and mortgages.

To calculate the amount you will need, first remember that you will, most likely, not pay taxes on this income, so the annual amount needed is less than the annual salary being made now. Take the current annual salary and deduct any taxes being paid. Multiply this amount by the number of years you want to provide this. Then add in any extra expenses that may be needed in the future, as listed above. This will be the benefit amount that you should obtain a policy for.

Life Insurance Chart

(Parentheses means subtraction)

Gross Annual Income ____________________

Taxes Paid Annually (____________________)

Total Annual Need = ____________________

Number of Years Coverage X ____________
Benefit Needed (1) = ____________

Future special expenses:
- mortgage balance ____________________
- business debts ____________________
- taxes (sale of business) ____________________
- college tuition ____________________
- funeral expenses ____________________
- medical bills ____________________
- estate taxes ____________________
- other ____________________

Total Other Expenses (2) = ______________

Total Annual Need (1+2) = ______________

Assets Available:
- cash/savings (____________)
- stocks (____________)
- 401k (____________)

Total Benefit Needed = ____________________

The Bottom Line

Once you have decided on what amount, what type, and who you will buy from, remember that you are the consumer. If you feel uncomfortable about the policy you just signed, you have a few days to change your mind — risk-free. Some states allow as many as 10 days for the free-trial period, while some have only 3 days. Ask when you talk to the agent or sales company.

Coverage You Didn't Know You Had

Many of us are covered for life insurance through credit card companies and jobs. The amount of the policy may not be much, but it is worth investigating. Many credit cards automatically cover you for $5000 of life insurance, and many employers cover their employees if they are killed while doing work (such as traveling on a business trip). This is in addition to the policies you purchase through the same employer.

Other sources of income when a spouse dies are Social Security (burial fee of $225) or veterans benefits (check with the Veteran's Administration to see if you qualify: 810 Vermont Ave, (40) NW, Wash D.C. 20420). If you are at least 60 years old and become widowed, you may collect on your husband. If you are a disabled widow, you can collect at age 50. If you are divorced and your marriage lasted at least 10 years, you may collect their Social Security when they die. Your children can collect Social Security if one parent dies —even if you are divorced.

MEDICAL INSURANCE

Nothing can wipe out your savings, current assets, and future plans faster than an uninsured medical situation. Unplanned medical expenses is the leading reason given for filing bankruptcy. A long stay in a hospital can cost $50,000 or more. This will throw your plans for retirement, savings, and even home ownership into chaos. It's not worth the risk.

I know of a family who said they couldn't afford medical insurance, so they didn't buy any. There was however enough money for accelerated educational programs and field trips. The mother of the large family had a freak accident and needed hundreds of thousands of dollars in care and surgeries. They asked others in their friendship circle and communities to help with costs. I understand that they needed help, but I questioned their lack of planning. Later, we'll look at affordable plans for families in tight times like this one.

Another reason to carry it is that you will always be treated better if you have insurance. Many doctor's and hospitals won't provide care, or will but with less quality and attention than their paying patients.

Where

When you decide what the right type of insurance is for you and your family, you should start doing some comparative shopping. The most accessible and the cheapest place to get insurance is through your employer or your spouse's employer. If you or your spouse have no employer policy available, other places to look are through any professional groups that you belong to, a college alumni association, your automobile insurance carrier, trade organization, military, clubs, credit card companies, AARP, or any school you may be attending. Buying a policy as an individual will cost you 15-40% more than being part of a group. If you are not a member of a group or trade organization, consider joining to get the group policy. If you are self-employed, membership in the National Association for Self-Employment (800-232-6273) offers a group discount.

If you are unhappy with the coverage available to you or you have some insurance coverage changes pending, check other alternatives.

Other Options

There are companies that cater to the individual instead of the group. These are worth looking into if you are self-employed or are not covered under any other group plan. Some even offer policies only for the kids. One company offers great coverage for a child for $35 per month. Examples of companies like this are Blue Cross Blue Shield, Mutual of Omaha, QualMed, Kaiser Permanente, etc.

You can purchase short-term policies to cover you during brief periods of change. These can range from 2-6 months and work much like traditional insurance policies, covering major medical needs, with deductibles and co-payments. These usually do not cover preexisting conditions.

There are high deductible policies that cost very little, and will cover you in the event of a costly emergency. These will not cover the daily medical needs, but will cover anything above $2500 or $5000. The monthly rate on these varies across the country, but would run from $85-$150 per month for a family of 4. This is better than the average independent comprehensive coverage policy costing $600 per month for a family. Most major medical companies offer these. If this is the route you take, buy directly from the carrier. It could save as much as 20% of the premium.

These high deductible policies are not to be confused with hospital indemnity policies. Those offer $100-$200 per day in hospital room charges. If you have an emergency, your fees will run closer to $900-$1000 per day. Get a comprehensive policy instead.

There are other options, many of which are offered by non-profit organizations. These are groups of people forming their own sharing groups for people that cannot afford regular insurance policies but want to be covered in case of a major medical illness or accident. These policies usually do not cover regular doctor appointments, but only major illness or injury. The groups usually require the member to be a professing Christian, adhere to a lifestyle as defined in the Bible, and attend church regularly. The members of these groups share the costs of other members' medical needs after a deductible is paid. The average cost per month for a family is $60-$210, depending on the amount of deductible chosen.

Here are a few of these groups:

SAMARITAN MINISTRIES
P.O. Box 413-Z
Washington, IL 61571-0413
http://home.spynet/John8-36/samaritan.htm
(309) 686-8868 ext. 232

CHRISTIAN MEDI-SHARE
(DIVISION OF THE AMERICAN EVANGELICAL ASSOCIATION)
P.O. Box 1779
Melbourne, FL 32902
http://www.tccm.org
(800) PSALM-23

CHRISTIAN BROTHERHOOD
http://www.cbnews/org
(800) 910-4226

For those who are not eligible for group plans elsewhere, and cannot afford an independent policy with full medical coverage on their own, this is a wise alternative. The lady in my earlier story who relied on the community to help her could have avoided the financial hardship by getting this type of policy.

If none of these appeal to you or fit your needs, check with local government agencies such as the state Medicare office. You can find your local office by checking in the phone book, or calling the federal Social Security Administration office for a local contact (800-772-1213).

Remember that if you are self-employed, a large portion of your health insurance premiums are tax deductible.

Switching

If you leave a job (other than being fired) you will most likely qualify for COBRA coverage (CONSOLIDATED OMNIBUS BUDGET RECONCILIATION ACT). COBRA is a federal law that requires an employer to offer employees and their dependents the opportunity to purchase continuation of health care coverage in certain circumstances when company-paid health benefits end. This allows you to continue the coverage you had for up to 18 months if the coverage cancellation was caused by layoffs, resignations, leave of absence or reduced work hours. If the loss of coverage was due to death of the employee, divorce, or dependent child becoming ineligible, then the coverage can continue up to 36 months. The premiums will be higher than you were paying because of the loss of the employee discount, but it may be cheaper than your alternatives.

When COBRA applies:

- *termination of employment*
- *leave of absence that results in a loss of coverage*
- *reduced work schedule that results in loss of coverage*
- *divorce*
- *child becoming an ineligible dependent*

COBRA may be a good choice if you are changing jobs, and have new insurance, but have either a waiting period, or a pre-existing condition that won't be covered for a period of time.

We used COBRA once when Beau's employer went out of business. He was unable to get another permanent job and was doing temporary work through agencies until he could find something permanent. We had just had a baby and needed medical coverage. After checking into an independent policy through our insurance carrier and Blue Shield, we found COBRA to cost us less.

Important Tips

- *COBRA will not be offered if employer has fewer than 20 people*
- *coverage in COBRA will cease if: a) You are late on a premium payment. b) You are eligible for COBRA due to a divorce, and you remarry. c) You become eligible under another group insurance plan due to employment. d) The employer providing COBRA ends the group plan for all employees*
- *converting to COBRA does not require waiting periods, qualifying for coverage, or exclusion of pre-existing conditions*
- *coverage sometimes covers less under COBRA — ask before sign-up*
- *your costs will be higher, since you have lost the group discount*

Types of Coverage

When I shop for insurance, the first thing I consider is the type of care I want. Ask yourself some questions. Is it important to you to have a doctor that you know and that you can always see each time you need to? Will you get the best testing done for a problem you encounter? Can you go where you think you need to? The answers to these will direct you to the type of carrier you should choose.

Traditional 80/20 — traditional coverage for services. Make sure you understand what is covered. *Disadvantages:* you pay the deductible out of your pocket, your portion of each visit is higher than an HMOs, and you have to deal with the billing paperwork. These type of plans usually have a deductible per person that must be paid out of your pocket before coverage begins, and then only 80% is covered. *Advantages:* you can pick the doctor of your choice.

Managed Care — you pay a flat monthly fee and choose a doctor from the provider's list. *Disadvantages:* because the insurance provider makes more money with less care provided to you, you may have to fight for the care you think you need. *Advantages:* because they want less major medical bills, they will emphasize preventative care more than the 80/20 type.

HMOs — like managed care, but you get a broader choice of doctors, and your fee includes a small co-payment for each type of coverage. *Disadvantages:* there are waiting periods for tests or specialists, since all must be approved by your primary physician. You are also limited as to the doctors you can use, and emergency room visits must be limited to life-threatening status or you may be charged for it. *Advantages:* more items are covered than through traditional coverage, there are no deductibles, preventative medicine is usually covered, the premiums are lower, and there is less paperwork.

PPOs— like managed care, it is a list of doctor's who have agreed to provide service at a fixed fee. You can use other doctors and pay a higher co-payment.

What to look for in medical coverage

- *inpatient hospital services*
- *surgical services*
- *ambulance coverage*
- *doctor office visits*
- *dependent coverage*
- *newborn coverage*
- *maternity care*
- *cesarean coverage*
- *annual exams/preventative care*
- *prescriptions*
- *laboratory work/tests*
- *x-rays*
- *physical therapy*
- *home health care if needed*
- *mental health coverage*
- *drug and alcohol abuse*

Who to Join

Many people make a superficial decision about which medical insurance carrier to choose. Some decide because they prefer the ease of a co-payment rather than submitting an insurance bill for refund. Our decision for our care should go beyond convenience. We should look at the type of care we'll receive, as well as the annual costs between carriers.

Some of the things to check for are:

Strength of the Company

Weiss Research will prepare research on the financial strength of most insurance organizations. A verbal report runs $15, with a one page brief costing $25, and a detailed 20 page report costing $45 (800-298-9222).

Patient Satisfaction

To check on how dissatisfied past patients have been with denials for coverage, etc., ask the HMO for their disenrollment rate. It should be below 15%.

HMO Services

To get other information and details on what an HMO offers, check out the free service called HMO SmartPages (http://www.buysmart.com/hmo).

Maximum Coverage per Lifetime

Preferably there is no maximum since a long illness can run that limit quickly. Seek out a company that has $1 million per person lifetime cap.

Deductibles

Are they per person or per family? Per family often is best if there are children. Pay as high a deductible as you can. You want to only pay for coverage of losses that you cannot afford. The higher the deductible, the lower the payments.

Duplicate Coverage

Make sure you do not pay for coverage twice: one for your spouse and one for yourself. Having a special policy for a disease and having comprehensive coverage is unnecessary (unless the comprehensive policy specifically excludes that disease). You can't be reimbursed twice for the same medical cost.

Exclusions

Some policies will not cover certain things. Check the fine print before signing. Typical exclusions are:

- *Pre-existing conditions: there is usually non-coverage and/or waiting periods for a pre-existing condition. A pre-existing condition can be defined as the existence of a symptom that a person received treatment within a five-year period. For example, a back injury from an earlier car accident may not be covered. HMO's typically offer better coverage for pre-existing coverage.*

- *substance abuse*
- *attempted suicide*
- *mental illness*
- *workers compensation claims*
- *cosmetic surgery*
- *pregnancy*
- *eyeglasses*
- *dental work*

Some people with preexisting conditions will never have to deal with exclusions, according to Clinton's Health Insurance Portability and Accountability Act of 1996. This act does not allow a new insurer to deny or delay coverage for a pre-existing condition if you were with a group plan for 18 months (or utilized COBRA for as long as you could) prior to signing on with another company.

Specialists

If anyone in your family has a condition that requires ongoing care from specialists (epilepsy, allergies, asthma, etc.), check if your insurance carrier has the kind of specialist that you need on the plan.

Cancelability

Check for cancelability of the policy. How much warning are they required to give you? For what reasons can they cancel your policy?

Renewability

This is usually a consumer right, but check and make sure. You don't want to lose coverage especially if you become ill and cannot get coverage for it with a new company.

Waiting Period

Is there any waiting period before you are covered?

Durable medical equipment

This includes wheelchairs, respirators, CPAP machines (for sleep apnea). Check the percentage paid by the carrier.

Which hospitals are covered

Make sure the institutions used have good records — not just the cheapest ones around.

Amount of Hospital Coverage

Some carriers only cover a certain dollar amount for the hospital room. That may be very insufficient, as rooms can cost up to $1000 per day. Make sure your policy covers a percentage of your room costs.

Emergencies

When is an emergency room visit covered? What about urgent care facilities? One type of service might be covered at a very different rate than the other. Also, some carriers restrict the coverage of certain types of visits to urgent care facilities and emergency rooms, and even might refuse to pay.

When you are ready to purchase medical insurance, estimate your potential medical needs. First, list what you needed last year. Then consider things such as the types of hospital services you may need: surgeries, prescriptions, ambulance, well baby care, maternity, physical therapy, out-of-town coverage, chronic illness coverage, and any annual cap on what you will spend. Then factor in the potential carrier's portion.

The chart on the next page is a comparison of some carriers that we evaluated. By doing this sort of evaluation, our family saved $300 per year.

Medical IQ

These are databases of medical literature (both traditional and alternative), including articles and journals with a wealth of information.

HEALTHWORLD..*HTTP://WWW.HEALTHY.NET*

GRATEFUL MED..*HTTP://GM.NLM.NIH.GOV*
(this service charges $2.40 per hour for use)

Insurance Company Comparison

EXPENSES PER YEAR	CARRIER A	B	C
Premium (family of 4)	*500*	*700*	*1000*
Deductible	*200*	*0*	*0*
Doctor's visits:			
2 kids annual exam	*30**	*0*	*0*
5 unplanned visits	*45**	*25***	*25***
Emergency (stitches, etc.)	*75**	*25****	*25****
Chiropractor (average 6 per year)	*60**	*300*	*150****
Medications (some won't cover certain drugs)	*20*	*100*	*100*
Annual Cost	*$930*	*$1150*	*$1300*

**20% is our portion*
***$5 co-payment per visit*
**** $25 co-payment per visit*

The Bottom Line

A few more things to remember when choosing insurance:

- Don't always assume that cheaper is better. Check the reputation of the carrier.
- Don't underinsure you or your family. Living without insurance is much like playing Roulette. The time will come when you need it.
- Consider your need (or lack of need) for accidental death insurance. You are more likely to become disabled than to die from an accident. Unless of course, you are very reckless. Also, heart attacks are not

considered an accident.

- Pay premiums on time! A lapse of premium makes a lack of coverage.
- Before having a procedure or surgery, check with the insurance company to make sure you are covered and have all proper pre-approval. You don't want to be hit with the surprise bill!

DISABILITY INSURANCE

The term "disabled" means that you are unable to perform your usual work for an extended period of time. If, after two years, you still have not returned to work, you qualify for Medicare.

Many people think that this type of insurance is more important than life insurance. A 30 year old has a 1 in 4 chance of being disabled for up to a year. Can you live on savings for a year? Disability insurance covers these things.

The benefit usually covers lost employment income. No policy pays for all lost income, but will rather pay for part of it. This provides an incentive for you to return to work. These benefits are usually tax free.

If you have many assets, insurers will be hesitant to provide you with disability insurance. They assume that you will not be motivated to return to work since you can live off of your assets. Working at home is also a concern for insurers as they cannot verify if you have returned to work or not.

To Save with Disability Insurance

- *increase the length of the waiting period before benefits begin, such as 90 or 180 days after loss of work; this can sometimes save as much as 25%*
- *reduce the percentage of salary benefits that you will receive once disabled*
- *shorten the length of time you will be covered*

Exclusions

The following things may not be covered by disability insurance:

- *suicide attempts that leave you unable to work, for physical or emotional reasons*
- *drug abuse that leaves you unable to work*
- *non-commercial plane crashes are not covered, unless you were on the ground and not in the plane*
- *military acts or war*
- *normal pregnancy since medical leave will usually cover this*

A minimum coverage of 60% of your income is recommended. Any less will be insufficient for your needs.

Where

One good source of disability insurance is USAA Insurance. They are highly rated by the Consumer Federation of America. You can find them at (800) 531-8080.

VISION

Many policies do not cover eye care, but we can't ignore this common problem. If vision insurance is too costly for you, consider paying for an exam yourself. There are inexpensive alternatives to an opthamologist exam which can cost up to $100 per year. An opthamologist is a complete doctor of the eye, treating both diseases of the eye as well as vision correction. Unless you have a serious eye problem, one alternative is to ask an optometrist to provide the exam and a prescription. An optometrist can screen and treat vision problems, but cannot treat diseases of the eye. Their fees are usually one fifth (1/5) what an opthamologist charges. Make sure that the exam is thorough, including an exam of the inner eye (done by dilating drops).

Another option is to check with your local health department who may provide free or very inexpensive exams. Also keep in mind that, unless you are elderly or have a serious eye problem, an annual exam is not necessary. Every 2-3 years is sufficient. They may also be able to provide inexpensive or free glasses.

Getting eye glasses also can be expensive. Don't feel obligated to use the services of your eye doctor for filling the prescription. Shop around. Some of the discount optometry chains that offer glasses give poor quality, while others have excellent reputations. Ask around, and call the Better Business Bureau for any complaints that may have been made.

For contact lenses, don't forget to look at mail order. These are an inexpensive and excellent alternative. Some companies are 1-800-CONTACTS, Factory Direct Lens (800-516-5367), and Contact Lens Discount Center (800-780-5367).

DOCTOR BILLS

When you do finally use the insurance carrier, find ways to reduce the expense of the doctor bill. Sometimes doctors act like it is a privilege to be seen by them, whereas we are actually hiring the doctor. And as with any work for hire, the fee needs to be discussed. Some doctors will write off your portion of the bill if you show financial need. Ask the carrier how you can reduce your part of the bill.

Below are some tips on how to reduce the doctor's bill:

- *If you are on an 80/20 plan and think your portion of the bill is too high, find out what an HMO would pay. Ask the doctor if you can pay what the HMO patient would have paid.*
- *Use the carrier's preferred doctors and save 40%.*
- *Use the phone as often as possible instead of making an appointment. Many doctors will advise you and even prescribe medication on the phone. You can save $50 and the hassle of an office visit by letting your fingers do the walking.*
- *See a general practitioner as often as possible over a specialist. They charge up to 40% less. Save the specialists for when it is necessary.*
- *Check out what your local county board of health has to offer. Many offer immunizations for children for free or for a minimal fee of $5. A visit to the doctor for the same service runs $75.*
- *Ask what the doctor charges. If you have a traditional 80/20 plan, this is essential. Not everyone charges the same rate. Rates can vary from $20 to $200 for an office visit.*

- *Avoid the emergency room. Use preventative care and common sense. Can it wait until the morning when the office opens? Can you talk with the doctor on the phone and get the advice you need to get through the night? If this will work, you can save hundreds of dollars off of the emergency room fee. (Many people don't have insurance so they don't go to a doctor until it turns into a major infection or problem. Then, they go to emergency care. This is more costly than going to a doctor and paying cash).*
- *Ask if the tests are necessary. What will they reveal? What alternatives are there to the test? Some doctors profit from the tests. For example if they have their own x-ray equipment, they tend to order 4 times more x-rays than if they used an outside service.*
- *Check around for a cheaper laboratory. I found a cheaper blood sugar screening (1/2 price) by calling all the ones covered by my plan.*
- *Don't let duplicate testing be done. Sometimes if you switch doctors or get a second opinion, they want to redo the tests with their lab. There is no reason for this unless there is something wrong with the quality of the first tests.*
- *Don't pay for a repeat of a test that wasn't your fault. For instance, if a lab loses a sample, and retesting is required, you do not have to pay again.*
- *Get a second opinion. If it's for surgery or a course of treatment that you question the necessity, the cost of another opinion will outweigh the cost of the wrong diagnosis.*
- *Read about home treatments. Many office visits can be avoided for ailments that the doctor can't do much about. Consider buying a medical guidebook. Check out a few from the library to see which one you like best.*

If you do get stuck with a fee that you didn't expect or cannot afford, try these time honored approaches:

- *tell the doctor of your circumstances*
- *ask about cash discounts; if you pay your portion at the time of service and don't wait to be billed, will they offer a discount*
- *will the doctor waive the co-payment*
- *will they take small monthly payments*

- *if you are going through a hard time financially, ask the doctor for a reduced fee; many would rather you get the care you need and be paid less, than have you go without care*

HOSPITAL BILLS

Hospital bills account for 40% of the amount spent in the US for health care. The best way to avoid the high cost of hospitalization is to make sure that you need to be there. Many surgeries are not necessary, or are subjective. Forty percent of hospital admittance was not necessary. Get a second opinion before committing to anything.

Often an admittance is to comfort and provide care that the patient may not get at home. Sometimes that is needed. But maybe there needs to be some reconsideration when the doctor says, "Let's check you in."

There are many ways that doctors handle medical situations. And it is important that we speak up if we think there may be a better way. One example of how different doctors work is when my husband had kidney stones. In California, each attack was treated as an outpatient basis. He was given pain killers in the emergency room, and then sent home until the stone passed, or he could get an appointment for the "stone crusher" (lithotripsy). We were often shuttling back and forth to the emergency room for better pain killers when the stone bothered him.

In Colorado, his attack warranted a 3 day hospital stay. They did nothing for him other than maintain the level of pain killer and make him comfortable. It was better for his comfort, but more costly. In order to meet aggressive health care cuts, California keeps you out of the hospital as much as possible. Births get you home in 24 hours, and kidney stones and most surgeries are done on out patient basis.

Questions You Should Ask Before Agreeing To Hospital Admittance

- *Can this be done as an outpatient?*
- *Will it be done as "open surgery" or as a minimally invasive surgery? The latter can usually be done as outpatient and requires less healing time.*
- *Can I be treated somewhere else (home heath care, nursing home)?*
- *Is surgery necessary? Are there other ways to treat this?*

Choosing a Hospital

For most of us, we can choose the hospital we want to go to. Unless our doctor is limited to one hospital or our insurance carrier limits us, we usually can make a choice. When choosing, we need to remember that not all hospitals offer the same fees, or quality of care. Both should be investigated.

Fees

The fees that hospitals charge vary greatly. Beau had two hospitalizations within the same town but with drastically different prices tags. His first stay was at a hospital in a lower income part of town. He stayed for 3 days in intensive care. That bill was $8000. He had another stay in a hospital in the nicer part of town for four hours in outpatient surgery, which had a price tag of $16,000.

It pays to check around for fees. Don't be afraid to call and ask. Teaching hospitals tend to be more expensive, and often are not covered by insurance companies. The city run or supported hospitals tend to be cheaper, but sometimes have poorer quality. To find these, ask where the police take accident victims or the uninsured.

Most people assume that a hospital bill is a fixed fee. In many cases it is, but this is not always the case. Many hospitals are very understanding and will accept whatever the insurance company will cover combined with whatever you are able to pay. To make this arrangement, you will need to plea your case and possibly offer documentation to support it. Many large bills can be negotiated, especially if the hospital is in a lower income area. These hospitals have many customers who just can't pay for their visit, so the hospital has to write off the cost. If a customer can pay, but needs to make small payments, they usually cooperate to get their money.

After my husband's stay in intensive care for 3 days, there were 12 different bills. We could only afford to pay each $10 per month. All of them were willing to accept these terms, and none ever charged interest. On the other trip to the hospital that cost $16,000, the hospital did not want to accept payments. Instead they offered us a 20% discount if we paid by the end of that month. That added up to a large savings, and was worth doing what we had to in order to pay them.

Don't be afraid to contest the amount that the insurance company decides to cover. There are humans with tender hearts working at these companies. I have had medications and procedures covered that normally would not, just because I wrote a sincere and explanatory letter regarding the situation. Send supporting documents, such as a doctor's letter, if you can.

Save 50% on Hospital Bills

Try an urgent care center before a hospital's emergency room, if you can. Urgent care centers may charge 50% less than hospital admissions.

Quality

Finding the right hospital can be as important as getting the right price. To find a good hospital in your area, ask your doctor's opinion.

You also can ask the hospital for it's track record — they know the average length of stay and the mortality rate for each type of illness and surgery.

Check out the Consumer's Guide to Hospitals published by the Center For The Study Of Services. It provides death rates, background information, and percentage of doctors that are board certified on many hospitals. It will tell you each hospital's death rate for each type of procedure you may need. Ask your librarian for this resource.

Check out the JCAHO (Joint Commission on Accreditation of Heathcare Organizations). They award accreditation to hospitals by evaluating guidelines for quality of care and services, procedures in intensive care, record keeping, and safety of equipment. Their question hotline is (630) 792-5000, or their main offices can be reached at (202) 434-4525.

Cutting Costs When Hospitalized

If you need to be at a hospital, have selected a hospital you are comfortable with, and know what to expect of the fees, there is one more step you can take. You can reduce some of the expenses while you are there. Try these to save a few dollars:

- *Check in and out according to their schedules. If you stay after the hospital's check out time, you will be charged an extra day, much like a hotel. The same goes for check in time. Find when their check in time is, and don't come before that. Billing usually is done by calendar days and not 24 hour periods.*
- *Avoid checking in on Fridays. Most hospital services are not available over the weekend, so you are paying for a few unnecessary days.*
- *Make sure your testing is not delaying your discharge. If you need a*

certain test in order to be discharged, and the lab is running late, you may be held another day for that test. Demand it be done in a timely manner, or ask the test to be done as outpatient the next day.

- *Bring your own linens (pillows, nightgown if allowed, slippers). These can run up to $300 per day! To save on these, you must inform the billing office of the hospital before you check in.*
- *Bring your own toiletries (shampoo, tissue, toothbrush, toothpaste, razors, etc.). A tissue box will run $4 and some razors have been charged $14.*
- *If you are on daily medication prior to admittance, bring your own so the hospital can't charge you a big mark up for filling your prescription.*
- *If you are waiting for a specialist to see you, or for a consultation between your regular doctor and another doctor he wishes to consult, don't let that delay keep you in. Call the consulting doctor's office if you need to speed things up.*
- *Ask questions. Why am I being discharged tomorrow and not today?*
- *Ask if pre-admittance tests are necessary. Some are routine and have nothing to do with your condition. If you need them, can they be done before going to the hospital? They are cheaper if you are not a patient of the hospital.*
- *Check in the day of surgery and not the night before, so another day's fee is saved.*
- *Check out as soon as possible. 10% of patients become ill at the hospital. There are many infections at a hospital.*

Finally

Review the bill carefully when it arrives—95% of hospital bills contain errors. Many of the errors are input mistakes, such as charging $110.00 for a pill, instead of $1.10. Ask for the bill to be itemized if it doesn't arrive that way. Review each charge and make sure you had that service or item done.

MEDICATIONS

Another area of savings is generic versions of prescription and over-the-counter drugs. This can save you 30-80% off the cost of name brand drugs. I have seen a drop from $100 to $20 for one prescription, due to the generic version of the identical drug. Even many over-the-counter drugs can have a large variance between a name brand and a generic version. In addition to using generic as often as possible, shop around. Many stores and warehouse clubs have varying rates for store brand versions of drugs.

I have heard of some people who won't buy generic brands, and insist only name brands be purchased. Some feel the generic version is not as good. But the law requires that the generic version have the same active ingredients as the original namebrand.

Others feel that the inventor of that item needs to encouraged to continue inventing new products. These shoppers feel if we buy the generic version, the inventors cannot afford to continue their good work. We must remember that no one stole the recipe for the generic version. Most generic drug formulas only come on the market after the original patent has expired. The original manufacturer holds this patent for many years (usually 10 years) and makes a great deal of profit from the formula before it is made public. Much of the original research was done independently, and then sold to a major manufacturer. So many of the big name advertisers didn't invent it. That manufacturer also sells much of its original product to the generic companies to be resold as a generic brand.

Don't overlook the mail order pharmacies, such as Medi-Mail (800) 331-1458, Action Mail Order (800) 452-1976, and America's Pharmacy (800) 247-1003. These are great for medications that you use regularly. They can give you a good discount, up to 60% off name brand prescriptions. If you have access to the AARP (American Association of Retired Persons), they also have arranged good pricing. Contact their pharmacy for details at (800) 456-2226.

For colds, I don't buy the all-in-one remedies that are advertised so heavily. You end up taking stuff that you don't need and paying for the convenience of having them combined. A bottle of decongestant with acetaminophen added will cost 20-30% more than if you buy them separately. Instead, know the ingredients and buy generically. Keep several separate bottles in the cabinet — one for each type of medication. I keep a piece of paper taped to the inside of the medicine cabinet that tells me what each ingredient is meant to help. When I have a certain symptom, I take that drug only. Some people like the heated medication drink (for flu) that is packaged for convenience. Take only what you need (fever reducer, decongestant, etc.) and have a hot cup of herb tea or hot water with lemon juice and honey. The same effect will be achieved and will cost you less. Below is the list taped to my cabinet, in hopes it will help you.

Generic Names and Purposes for Cold Medications

dextromethorphan	*for dry cough/ cough suppressant*
guaifenesin	*for gooey cough/expectorant*
pseudoephedrine	*decongestant*
phenylpropanolamine	*decongestant*
ephedrine	*decongestant*
chlorpheniramine	*antihistamine*
diphenhydramine	*antihistamine*

It's important to know what you need. You can complicate your problems by using the wrong drug. For example, if you have a gooey cough, using a cough suppressant isn't a good idea. Ask your doctor or pharmacist before you self-medicate to be sure you're choosing the right medicine.

With any medication, compare the unit price per amount of ingredients (the cost per milliliter or milligram). Sometimes it's cheaper to take 2 capsules of a lesser dose than one pill of a larger dose. This is particularly true of aspirins and other pain killers. Again, you are paying for the convenience of someone combining pills for you.

Other Ways to Save

- *Are you popping pills all the time? Look into the cause of the trouble. Is it poor nutrition, an imbalanced diet, inadequate daily water intake, or something more serious that requires a doctor's attention?*
- *Look into an alternative way of treating the problem. Other approaches include: nutritional, chiropractic, exercise, support groups, etc. Do research from all angles before resigning to drugs. Doctors won't encourage you to pursue alternative avenues because they are not trained or experienced in them.*
- *Consult a medical guide for treating yourself for common ailments.*
- *Sometimes alternative medicine is not as wise as seeing a doctor and taking prescriptions. It may be causing a larger problem. I know people who try to cure strep throat naturally. I think that is great if it works. But some people keep on "getting it back." Strep throat is nothing to mess with, since it can develop into rheumatic fever if not treated. A simple dose of penicillin is less harmful to your body and less costly than heart damage.*
- *Take advantage of senior citizen discounts. You qualify at age 55.*
- *Shop at discount drug stores. This can save up to 40%.*
- *When buying over-the-counter drugs, buy the largest container size that you would consume over a 6-month period. This will save you 35%.*

Tips for Kids

Since chewable medicine is more costly than tablets, try these savings tips:

- *crush an adult tablet of the drug (make sure it's cut to the child's dose first) and mix with honey or jam*
- *getting kids to swallow a pill is helpful, have them practice by swallowing M&Ms or Tic-Tacs — mistakes aren't nasty tasting*

Free Drugs

There are some free things that are easy to obtain. Many doctors are given free drugs as samples by the pharmaceutical companies. They are meant to be given to patients. Ask for them.

For those who cannot afford their prescriptions, the Pharmaceutical Manufacturers' Association offers free medications. Eligibility requirements vary. Some drug manufacturers have strict financial hardship requirements, while others leave it to the doctor's discretion. Whichever is used, a doctor must certify the patients medical need for the drug, and apply for you to the PMA. If your doctor is unfamiliar with this program, give him/her the PMA phone number (800-PMA-INFO).

Don't Save This Way

Don't try and save by not taking all the prescription in hopes of using it later. You may end up with a secondary problem that will cost more than the bottle of pills. For example, by not completing a course of antibiotics, you run the risk of building an immunity to that antibiotic, and having complications the next time you are sick. Even if you feel better you need to finish the bottle.

Don't take over the counter drugs if your symptoms persist. See a doctor before your condition becomes really serious and costly.

Check the expiration date on medicines. Some get stronger with age, while others weaken. Discard (flush down the toilet) expired medications.

DENTAL EXPENSES

Many people avoid going to the dentist. Not only because it's an uncomfortable encounter, but because many people are not covered by health

insurance that includes a dental plan. Many employers can't afford dental insurance, thus leaving the people on their own. Since they have to pay for all visits out of their own pockets, they tend to avoid preventative care and wait until it's too late or too costly to save a tooth.

There are several dental plans available to the average person. Some are under $100 per year, and work like an HMO with you choosing from their selected dentists. These plans usually pay 100% of preventative care (cleanings, checkups, and basic fillings). Many department stores are offering these (Sears, Montgomery Wards). There are also plans through Medicaid and Medicare.

Whether you can afford dental insurance or not, here are some ways to make the most of your dental budget:

Prevention

As much as I hate to admit it, the dentists are right: prevention is the best way. By brushing after meals, flossing, avoiding sugar and getting regular cleanings, we prevent plaque from eating the enamel and causing expensive cavities or root canals. I know this because I did not practice good dental care until a few years ago. And now I am paying for it. I don't mean that I was not brushing and flossing. I was doing both, but either at the wrong times or not frequent enough. Most of us eat between meals without brushing. And many of us do not floss every night. When I learned that 35% of all gum disease and tooth loss comes from plaque destroying teeth, I took notice. A root canal can cost $250 per tooth. You can buy a lot of dental floss and brushes for that. You can also save yourself some gum and enamel damage by using the right kind of brush and by brushing correctly. Follow your dentist's instructions.

You don't need a name brand toothpaste to have healthier teeth. You also can use less paste than television commercials suggest. When I grew up overseas, we could not get toothpaste. We could order tooth powder, but when we ran out, we used the healthy standby — baking soda and salt. You can mix it with cinnamon, mint extract, or a flavored fluoride liquid to enhance the flavor. This is healthy for the teeth and gums and very cheap.

The whole idea of brushing is to keep the foods (particularly sugar) off of the teeth so plaque isn't encouraged to grow. So, if you brush, don't snack immediately. When you brush in the morning, do so after breakfast. The same principle applies to our kids. Don't let them snack or drink juice or milk all day. After they eat a meal, brush their teeth. Snacks should be nonsugar items such as vegetables and water. Make sure they go to bed with clean teeth and no bottles or cups of juice or milk. The constant bath of juice (or milk) on their teeth eats away at the enamel. All of this may sound excessive, but it saves teeth and money.

Cleaning

The best preventative care is to have a professional cleaning twice a year. Plan for this in the budget. It is much cheaper than a root canal or extraction. Another possible expense is braces later due to a drifting bite from the missing tooth.

To save on the professional cleanings, try a local dental school or community college. They charge as much as 75% less than a private dentist. Many county health departments also have dental facilities.

Dental & Orthodontic Work

Dental or orthodontic care also can be obtained at local universities and dental schools. Some offer low-cost appointments by students in training. These students always are supervised by certified dentists. The cost of an average visit is 50% less than a similar visit to a dentist in private practice. If you cannot afford much at all, check with your local county health department for low cost dental services.

Other Ways to Save

- *Having x-rays done annually is not necessary, says the American Dental Association. Unless there is a suspected problem, x-rays for the entire mouth are needed only every 3 years.*
- *Consider sealants for molars. They cost $20-$50 per tooth, but protect against cavities for up to 10 years. Fillings cost more than this and usually have to be replaced.*
- *Brushing the correct way with a good toothbrush is as effective as an electric or ultrasonic toothbrush, and costs less.*
- *Don't wait until something hurts to have it fixed. Most problems don't hurt until it's too late and requires expensive solutions.*

Don't Save This Way

If you need special work done, such as a root canal, get a referral to a specialist (in this case, an endodontist). Paying the higher fee for a specialist to do the job is worth the cost versus the risk of an improper job. Someone who doesn't do the work correctly can cause cracked teeth or years of struggle with nerve damage and pain.

CHAPTER SEVEN

Help Around the House Electronics & Appliances

I think housework is the reason most women go to the office.

–Heloise, 1963

Gotcha! You probably thought that I was going to tell you how to get free maid service. After all, the Proverbs 31 woman in the Bible had handmaidens. Many people believe that is the only way she could do all that she did. Maybe — but maybe you have the same help too.

Some of us have a romantic notion of the olden days, where our ancestors had leisurely teas and strolls to the neighbors for a visit in the parlor. Many families have lived in this manner, but most did not. Even those who had these luxuries, did it with help. Someone else did the wash, cooking and cleaning, milking of the cow, churning of the butter, and making of the clothes. The handmaidens of that day.

Servants seem like such a luxury to us. But back then it was standard. Household budgets included their wages just like our budgets include a washer, dryer or refrigerator. As families tired of unreliable help, home appliances were invented — mostly in America.

At first, only the rich could afford these bulky machines. As they improved and more models were produced, the prices came down. Servants were replaced with electronic handmaidens.

Even though our current day handmaidens are more electronic in nature, they are just as valuable to us. They give us the freedom to do the other things in life, just like our ancestors did. Let us not forget how much work they had, or we would have, if we lived without our handmaidens:

We don't chop the wood then stoke the fire to make breakfast
We flick the switch on the stove.

We don't milk the cow and churn the butter
We drop into the local market.

We don't drag the carpet out and beat it
We vacuum it.

We don't draw water from a pump, well or river
We turn on a faucet.

We don't sew all of our clothes — including underwear
We drop into a department store.

We don't draw 10 gallons of water from the pump, drag it to the back yard tub, start a fire, boil the clothes, hang them, and redye the faded ones
We have a washer and dryer.

We don't dry, cure and store our foods for the winter
We drop into the local store.

We don't clean chamber pots every morning
We flush.

We don't spend 1/5 of our waking hours doing dishes
We have a dishwasher.

Now that we understand the origin and value of our electronics, let's see how we can afford buying them.

Helpful Household Hotlines

CLOTHING
800-435-6223
http://www.helmac.com
advice on removing stains and general clothing care

CARPET
800-882-8846
http://www.carpet-rug.com
advice on types of fibers to buy, maintenance and cleaning

LEATHER
800-852-3876
advice on care of leather furniture

PORCELAIN
615-385-5357
http://www.porcelainenamel.com
advice on cleaning porcelain and enamel surfaces

BUYING ELECTRONICS

Buying electronics can be overwhelming. The sales people think you should buy one model, your family wants another, and you favor a different one. Who do you listen to? This section is not suppose to be a consumer guide on which model to buy of which device. There are plenty of those around. Rather, it is my hope that this is a guide of steps to follow before making decisions.

These steps can be applied to almost any item you are purchasing. Basically, three decisions need to be made: know what you want, research the choices, and decide to buy new or used.

1. Know what you want

- *List all the features essential to you. If you shop based on what looks nice or seems good, you will regret your decision later. Ask yourself if the new frig needs spill proof shelves, auto defrost or an ice maker before you shop. Does that washing machine need multi-speed settings or is the plain version satisfactory? Does the video camera need to be VHS or is it okay to have 8 mm?*

- *If you are unfamiliar with the product you are buying because you have never used one regularly, ask people who do use them. A good example is cell phones. More and more people are buying them, but many have never owned or used them before. In this case, talk to people who have had them awhile. What do they wish they had or didn't have? What features did they later find were essential, or perhaps unnecessary? What aspects of the service contract did they overlook? Learn from their mistakes.*
- *Measure the space it will take before you buy. Sometimes an appliance doesn't fit after being delivered. Also check the compatibility of the features to the place it will occupy. You don't want to find there is room for the clothes dryer, but not its vent hose. Or that the new television may fit in the cabinet, but its speakers on the sides are now blocked by wood.*

2. Research the choices

Once you know what features you want, check for who makes it best.

- *list all the companies that make the appliance are want to buy*
- *check consumer magazines at the library for reliability ratings on each manufacturer and model*
- *create a spread sheet or grid of this information so it is easy to see who rates best (see example below)*

Example of a Grid for Comparison Shopping:

	MANUFACTURER A	MANUFACTURER B	MANUFACTURER C
MODEL A			
safety	*pass*	*fail*	*good*
service	*fail*	*pass*	*pass*
overall	*pass*	*pass*	*good*
MODEL B			
safety	*fail*	*pass*	*good*
service	*pass*	*pass*	*pass*
overall	*good*	*fail*	*fail*
MODEL C			
safety	*pass*	*good*	*fail*
service	*pass*	*pass*	*pass*
overall	*good*	*pass*	*pass*

3. Used or New?

Many thrifty folks buy used appliances and electronics because they are more affordable. I can relate. When we moved to Colorado, all of our major appliances stayed with the house in California—a package deal. That meant we had to buy a washer, dryer and refrigerator. The first thing we looked at was used machinery because of the sheer enormity of the cost. But after taking a closer look, we began to wonder if we needed to save more and buy new models.

Part of the problem we encountered was the used equipment was often very old and the company selling them was questionable as to reputation and reliability to fix broken items. When we looked in the paper for individuals selling appliances, their prices were not too much less than new—maybe $75 less. But an individual cannot offer a warranty that the item would work once we got it home. We felt the risks of a used model outweighed the savings. For a bit more, we could get a new one with a warranty.

Also factor the cost of running the appliance. The new models are so energy efficient, that overall they cost less to own. Appliances as young as three years old use up to three times more energy than the new ones. We checked into the models' energy consumption and factored that in with the purchase price. We came out way ahead with a new one. Here's our chart on the long term cost of a refrigerator from 1990, 1993 and 1996:

Energy Consumption Chart

Model Year	*Annual Energy Cost*	*Purchase Price Today*	*Cost in Five Years (price + energy use)*
1990	*$300*	*$150*	*$1650*
1993	*$166*	*$400*	*$1230*
1996	*$ 60*	*$500*	*$ 800*

Not everyone would agree with my decision. Many can get a more dramatic deal on a used model. Others may not be able to save and wait for the extra money needed to get a new one instead of a used one. If you fall into any of these categories, here are some tips to keep in mind if you are shopping for a used electronic item.

If Buying Used...

- *Make sure the model has a good reliability rating. Check at the library for information on older models—their service record and general overall satisfaction rating given by consumers. Some publications that carry this information are Consumer Digest and Consumer Reports.*
- *If you are buying the item from a store, call your local Better Business Bureau and get the scoop on the store. Have they had complaints against their service and products? Skip buying from them, no matter how good the deal.*
- *If the store checks out, make sure the unit has a warranty.*
- *If you are buying from an individual, ask that they be willing to take the unit back if it does not work within one week of delivery. Many appliances act funny once unplugged and moved.*
- *Allow for delivery costs of the item. Unless you have a truck or a friend who has one and is willing to help you, you may have to add $50 or more to the purchase in order to get it home.*
- *Check the energy rating. If it rates high, the model may actually cost more in a few years than a new model would. If this is the case, it would be cheaper to save and buy a new one.*

If Buying New...

Sometimes used models just aren't the best buy. Watching sales on new items can sometimes be a more lucrative decision. Here are some more tips on buying new electronics:

- *Look (and ask) for blemishes or superficial defect models. When we decided to buy new models, the cash was very tight. We watched sales and saved our pennies for months and found the best price we could. We went ready to buy a plain refrigerator that was advertised. When we got there we learned that there were some models on the* *floor that had cosmetic defects, such as paint scratches. These were marked off an additional $150. We were able to get a new model for not much more than what a used one would have been.*

- *Know what a good sale price is. Small appliances such as dishwashers or microwaves have a mark up of 30%. So a good sale should be 30% off retail. Larger appliances such as refrigerators and dryers have a mark up of 15%.*

- *Shop for the models that are tops in your research. One tip for better pricing is to get a copy of the Sunday newspaper from a major city in the US (you can get these at libraries and bookstores). Look for the electronics flyers and compare prices on the same make and model as your local flyers offer. If it is the same model and manufacturer, you can ask your local retailer to match that lower price. Good cities to read the Sunday paper are New York City (The New York Times), Los Angeles (The LA Times), and Chicago (The Chicago Tribune).*

- *Call the manufacturer and get the model numbers for last year's discontinued models. Ask at the department store to see if any of these models are left (at a good discount price), or use this model number at the mail-order outlets (see below).*

- *Consider some of the mail-order outlets. They offer goods at good discounts and offer full warranties that will be honored by most local repair centers. To use these, you need to know the exact manufacturer name, model number and description. A few that carry appliances are listed on the next page.*

CRUTCHFIELD—*COMPUTERS, VIDEO CAMERAS, PHONES AND FAX EQUIPMENT, AUDIO EQUIPMENT FOR HOME AND AUTO*
1 Crutchfield Park
Charlottesville, VA 22906-6020
(800-955-9009)
http://www.crutchfield.com/

EBA WHOLESALE— *major appliances of more than 50 namebrands*
(888-728-3266)
http://www.eaw-inc.com/index.html

BERNIE'S DISCOUNT CENTER—*all types of electronics and appliances*
821 Sixth Ave
New York, NY 10001
(212-564-8582)
http://www.advantageresource.com/appliancesmall.htm

FRUGAL FIVE: Electronics

$$$$$	Department Stores
$$$$	Sale at department stores
$$$	Sale at department store, blemished
$$	Rebuilt/thrift store
$	Used/second hand

CHAPTER EIGHT

Furnishing Your Home

The only really good place to buy lumber is at a store where the lumber has already been cut and attached together in the form of furniture...

—Dave Barry, "The Taming of the Screw"

Furnishing a house can be very expensive. Especially when there are so many details. In addition to the big ticket items such as couches and tables, there are lamps and end tables, headboards and foot boards, and so much more. But making a house look homey and warm doesn't have to cost a fortune, or require a second income. With a little resourcefulness and creativity, a little cash can go a long way.

We know first hand what it's like to start from scratch. Before Beau and I were married, we had always each rented rooms in furnished homes. When we married and found our own place, it was not furnished. For a bed, we spread the sheet on the floor at night. A friend lent us their foam camping pad until we saved enough for a mattress. That laid on the floor until we were able to move my old furniture from my parent's house into our apartment. For a table, we borrowed a rickety card table from a friend and some metal folding chairs from the church. If you cut anything firm, the table wobbled. One person had to hold the table while another cut. For the television stand, we covered an old trunk with a cloth. We eventually furnished the apartment by saving and looking for sales (the mattress), garage sales (the dining table) and asking if anyone had spare furniture (my mom's old couch). Hard work, creativity and resourcefulness.

WHERE TO BUY

There are many places to buy home furnishings, including department stores, estates sales, and thrift stores. And some families go even further and make their furniture themselves. We have done each of these things at one time or another throughout our marriage. Let's walk through each type of purchase.

Department Stores

Department stores and furniture stores can be a great place to buy furniture if you know what you are looking for and how to buy. Knowing what you need and want is the most important step. Do you need a love seat or full size couch, a 6-8 seat table or a kitchen table. What are the measurements for the space it will live in? If you don't know exactly what you need, you will end up buying more than necessary.

Once you have a shopping list, start watching sales. Many of the sale items are great deals. Many are not. To know if you have a good deal or not, figure what their profit is. A furniture store makes $55 on every $100 of the full retail price. So the sale price should be at least 40% off of retail to be a good price.

Whatever you buy, make sure the pieces are manufactured well (see the section below on Tips For Buying). If buying from a department store, make sure there is a warranty against manufacturing defects (such as broken internal frames, tearing fabric, excessively wearing fabric, etc.). Also try and have delivery included. That will save you a backache.

Outlet Stores

There are furniture outlet stores that cater to the public. These are no frills warehouses that have a few samples on display and you order from these. For people who live in smaller cities, this is a great way to get a lower price. These places are good sources for large furniture items, as long as you can get the warranty and check the quality of the construction on the demo models.

Mail Order

Other outlet centers are available to anyone in the USA — by mail. They offer any name brand furniture at 30-50% off retail. These folks have the goods but don't have expensive overhead, so they sell directly to you at less. Shipping the furniture adds very little to the overall price. In order to buy from them, have the manufacturer's name, model number, size and any other details you would need (color, type of finish on the wood). Here are a few of these type of stores:

CEDAR RACK FURNITURE
Box 515
Hudson, NC 28638
(704) 396-2361

QUALITY FURNITURE MARKET
2034 Hickory Blvd. SW
Lenoir, NC 28645
(704) 728-2964

BLACKWELDERS' INDUSTRIES—carries various manufacturers and charges minimal fee for catalogs
Route 18, Box 8
Stateville, NC 28677
(800) 438-0201

FURNITURE CHOICES
2501 Peters Creek Parkway
Greensboro, NC 27107
(910) 720-9700

DESIGNER SECRETS
P.O. Box 529
Fremont, NE 68025
(800) 955-2559

Many of the furniture manufacturers are located in North Carolina. One place they congregate is the Hickory Furniture Mart. There are hundreds of retailers plus a few manufacturer's represented. To get a listing of all of them, call their general number (800-462-MART) or write:

Hickory Furniture Mart
2220 Highway 705E
Hickory, NC 28601

If you would like a comprehensive list of furniture mail-order companies, buy (or look at the library) The Wholesale-By-Mail Catalog ($15, HarperCollins).

Some manufacturers will let you order directly by phone. This cuts out the retailer and saves you plenty. Once you know the manufacturer of the item, call for their 800 number (800-555-1212) and contact them.

Become Your Own Decorator

By obtaining a business license and resale number from your city, you can buy furnishings directly from manufacturers at a great discount. You can also make arrangements directly with custom laborers, cutting out the middle man.

Thrift Stores

Thrift stores can be filled with treasures if you know how to look. In order to find the best goods, you have to visit the thrift shops frequently. Their products turn over often as new stuff is donated daily and older items are sold. Find out which days donations are taken. Shop those days. You will get the best items this way.

By the way, many thrift shops have "bag days." This is when you pay a flat fee for a bag filled with items. This is a great time to buy. I know a lady who "hit" a bag day when they were selling dolls. She got three grocery bags filled with various types of dolls, including Barbies and large dolls, for only a few dollars. This has little to do with furnishing your home, but I thought you'd enjoy the tip.

Garage Sales

Another treasure hunt can be garage sales. These can harbor gold mines, or garbage dumps. Some ways to assure that you find gold are:

- *shop early—later in the day means less selection*
- *be fair in your offers; here are some guidelines:*
  - *–housewares and clothing items should be around 1/10th of their retail value*

–larger items such as furniture or appliances should be 1/2 of their retail value.

- *make a list of the sales you want to visit; plan them out on a map*
- *search behind items since others may be hiding*
- *check carefully for damage—pick up the item and scan all surfaces; ask to plug it in and operate if electrical*
- *barter—think of the maximum that you will pay and offer a bit less to start*

There are numerous success stories of families furnishing their homes with quality products found at garage sales. I have seen people sell excellent appliances for pennies on the dollar. Dressers bought for $10, designer dishes for $5 a set, headboard with mattress and box springs for $20, etc. We found a solid maple dining table with 6 chairs for $75. We still have it today (17 years later!) Families who have furnished their homes with these treasures have been featured in newspapers and books. Their homes are lovely, and not cheap looking. With a little determination, you can have a lovely home on a shoestring.

Making Your Own

Aside from bargain hunting at garage sales and watching advertisements, there is one other way to save in this area. One family I know builds their own furniture—for free. They find furniture manufacturers or staircase makers, and take the scraps of wood left from their projects. Usually the wood is given for free, as long as they pick it up. My friends' latest project is an armoire entertainment center. It is made of solid oak scraps, obtained for free. The total cost was less than $20 for hinges and supplies.

HOW TO BUY

Tips For Buying Furniture

Buying furniture that is made from wood requires that you make sure it is real wood first. Check the top of the piece first. If it is formica it will be dull and have a very smooth surface. Ask if the wood is veneer (a thin layer of real wood attached to particle board or cheap wood underneath). If it is, you want to avoid it. Veneer can chip easily. If the item is made from real wood, the finish can be re-stained, so don't be put off by marks. Deep gouges or burns, however, cannot be sanded away. Small scratches can be covered with stain or wax. Watermarks can be removed from real wood by stripping the finish and applying oxalic acid, then refinishing.

Once you have checked the quality of the wood and its finish, now you need to check on the quality of the construction.

For tables, the legs should be stable and not wobble, and the corners should be glued and screwed into place. We bought some wooden chairs at a garage sale that had joints that were glued and not screwed. We constantly had trouble with breaking and reglueing parts for years.

For cabinets and dressers, joints should be dovetailed (interlocking wood) and not only nailed. Legs should not be screwed in this case. Any hardware such as handles or knobs should be joined by screws. Drawers should have guides and stops.

Sofas and couches are only as good as the frame they are constructed around. Find out, if you can, what type of wood it was made of and how the frame was built. Check the external part of the frame for screws and bolts (which should not be what is holding it together). Soft woods, such as pine, will break sooner. Also try and find what types of spring and foam are used. Certain types of foam break down quickly, creating a sinking effect when you sit down. The cheaper the foam, the sooner it will break down. A low quality cushion foam can be replaced by buying high density foam and wrapping it in polyester fiber before covering it. You should be able to exert pressure on the arms of a chair and not feel any thing give. Feel for springs in the cushions and check underneath for exposed springs.

Mattresses come in three types: solid, foam, and innerspring. Solid means it has no springs but is made of filling and padding. These are good for bunk beds and rollaways. Foam mattresses are large slabs of foam covered by a mattress. Innerspring mattresses have coils in them. Better quality mattresses will have lots of springs. A good mattress will quickly return to its original shape after you get up. The edges should not be worn, and you should not be able to feel the coils when you press on the mattress. Box springs should have a row of wood under each row of springs.

REUSING WHAT YOU HAVE

Creativity

Before you throw something out or look to purchase something, think of what you can do with what you have. Recover an old worn sofa. Reuse that old sheet for something else.

If you have a fine sofa, but the material has had it from all those little feet and spilled drinks, here is a creative idea. Take some material that you like and recover it. For this, you can again use a sheet, or buy a heavier fabric at an upholstery fabric outlet store. They have the ends of the fabric rolls that furniture stores used. Attach the fabric to the existing seams with a staple gun. Remove the fabric in sections with a razor edge and use them as the pattern (add 2 inches to each side for tucking and mistakes). Our love seat cost $60 to recover myself. I was quoted $500 to have it recovered professionally.

Here are some other creative decorating tips:

- *a child's old potty or old BBQ kettle can become a plant container*
- *make a bed ruffle with 3-4 yards of fabric and attach to an old sheet*
- *decorate walls with stenciling*
- *pretty table cloths can be draped as swags over windows*
- *make a mirror out of an old picture frame*
- *make tables or benches from old doors*
- *fill antique shoes with dried flowers*
- *use an old wheelbarrow as a magazine rack*
- *use an old jug for the base of a lamp*
- *use a colorful blanket for a curtain*
- *recover the cushions on your sofa or throw pillows*
- *perk up a tired lamp with lace or notions*
- *brighten a curtain rod with gold or silver spray paint*
- *add a mirror to a small room to make it seem larger*
- *use old clothing to sew other things with:*
    - *throw pillow*
    - *quilts*
    - *basket liners*

dish towels

braided rugs (wool)

placemats

coasters

drapes

guest towels

Kid's Playhouse Idea

My sister-in-law, Terri, creatively turned a hall closet into a playhouse for her grandson. She put a chalkboard on one wall, a pretend pay phone on the other wall, shelves for toys, a table and chair and a lamp. My kids had more fun in that "house" when we visited. A little creativity goes a long way!

FRUGAL FIVE: Furniture

$$$$$	Department store sales
$$$$	Estate sales
$$$	Thrift Stores
$$	Garage sales
$	Make it yourself

CHAPTER NINE

Car Buying

A purpose without a plan is pitiful.

–*Ronald & Barbara Sennert,* How To Save $9000 On Your Next Car Or Van

FIRST ASK YOURSELF, "Do I really need a car?" or, "Do I really need another car?" Probably most people do need at least one car. Unlike Europe, much of which has excellent mass transport systems, most of North America does not have even adequate public transportation. This is partly because of sheer size, and partly because the vast majority of the population of this area of the world, unlike Europe, developed after the invention of the automobile. Unless you live in an urban or suburban area, close to work, schools, shopping, etc., you will find a car indispensable.

But do you need another car? The two-car family may be an American tradition, but many families manage fine with only one car. Since a car is the third biggest expense a family incurs after housing and insurance, families on a tight budget would be wise to consider very carefully whether they really need two cars.

There are many issues involved in buying, keeping, and maintaining a car. Some of these include the following: should it be a new or used car? Is it smarter to pay cash or finance it? Should I lease or buy? Can I afford the higher insurance of this car? Will this new car have a higher insurance rate?

Do I want a foreign or domestic car? Should I sell my present car or trade it in? How do I know which cars are most reliable? Cheapest to operate and maintain? Safest?

National Character of Cars

An interesting fact about cars seldom thought about is that each country manufactures its cars along certain lines and with particular values in mind. For example, German cars are noted for their overall performance (Porsche, BMW). Italian cars have a certain spirit (Ferrari, Lamborgini). The Swedes are known for building the safest cars (Volvo, Saab). The French make exotic cars (Citroen). The British make racy cars (Jaguar, Aston Martin). Japanese cars are known for value and reliability (Nissan, Toyota, Honda). Korean cars are inexpensive (Hyundai, Kia). Most American cars are practical (Chevrolet, Ford). Since a car is in some ways an extension of your personality, you might want to think about which aspects of a car are most important to you.

Value in Cars

As in most material things, value in cars is subjective. What a college kid on a limited income regards as value will likely be a lot different than that of a middle class mom of five. The college kid is looking for basic transportation; the mom of five needs lots of space and quite a bit of practicality. People who spend much time in their cars, such as traveling salesmen, will rate comfort and reliability as important values.

Another thing to consider when trying to determine a particular car's value is to think of value in terms of the total life of the car. If you plan to keep your car for a long time — say eight to ten years, or 150,000 miles or more — you will probably want a car that not only has an excellent reputation for durability but also is noted for low cost maintenance. Fuel consumption should also be taken into consideration. If you are planning on having a car for a shorter time, resale value might be a major factor. Some cars retain their value much better than others, and that could mean more money at trade-in time.

These Are the Good Old Days

Fortunately, for today's shopper looking to buy a car, these are the good old days. Cars today are more powerful, cheaper to run, more comfortable, safer, and more fun to drive. For example, it used to be that only the most expensive sports cars could deliver the performance that a number of today's sedans deliver routinely — and without being gas hogs. Seats are more comfortable, driving positions more natural, visibility better. Today's cars brake better, corner better, accelerate better, last longer, have better paint and finishing, and often are less costly to repair.

A good deal of this is probably a result of the excellence foreign manufacturers have brought to the North American car market. After all, in the United States, for more than a decade, it has usually been a foreign car that has been the best selling car. This has spurred American car makers to put a better product on the market, and the competition with foreign companies has had the effect of raising the bar for the entire industry.

Buying a New Car

Unless you're one of the few people who love to haggle, buying a car will probably cause you some anxiety. Even if you don't mind a little wheeling and dealing, you're probably still going to come out the loser when you go up against a car dealer. They are experts at it and you're not. Haggling is what they do for a living — and that's not what most of us spend all day long doing. They know every trick of the trade — not all of them completely above board — and they're perfectly prepared to use them on you, the unsuspecting victim.

One of the ways you can even the playing field is to go in prepared. For example, there are resources that will tell you the dealer invoice of any car you may want to buy. (For a list, see the resources box towards the end of this chapter). Most car dealers will settle for somewhere around $500 above invoice, which is often thousands of dollars less than the sticker price. Edmunds Consumer Information (see listing toward end of chapter) on car buying recommends a formula for figuring a fair car price: DEALER INVOICE + OPTIONS – REBATES + 5% PROFIT + DESTINATION FEES + TAX.

Be thoroughly knowledgeable about financing. Know your interest rate and what you can get elsewhere before discussing financing. You can probably get a better deal elsewhere. Car dealers often make their biggest profits on financing and warranties. In fact, most car dealerships have a special department called finance and insurance (F & I). Their job is to convince you to buy their products, which are often marked up 300% or more, or, in the case of financing, are several points above market value. Know what you are covered for by your current insurance agent before going into their insurance carrier's office. Often the car dealers offer what looks like a great deal but it covers nothing important.

Some of their offerings include hundreds of dollars for rust proofing, which all cars already have; fabric protection, which is simply about $10 worth of Scotchguard for which you pay a couple hundred of dollars; pin striping which costs $300 or $400 and worth about one-third that; gold trim, which isn't gold at all but anodized aluminum; extended warranties which cover items already covered by factory warranty. One car dealership had a neat scam: they had a built-in additional warranty as part of their invoice. When they asked buyers if they wanted the extra warranty and they declined, it was left in the invoice. If buyers accepted it, they were charged double.

Another trick car dealers often use is to try and get buyers' minds off what the price of the car is and on to what their monthly payment will be. If they can get customers to say what they want to pay a month, they can play around with financing figures, giving the buyer low payments, but still insuring that they make a large profit in the end.

Before making a final decision on any car, test drive the vehicle. There are many things to check in your test drive, so it is best if you can get the dealer to let you have the car for an extensive period of time. After all, you are spending quite a bit of hard-earned money to buy a new car, and you will be spending a good deal of time in it. You should have the opportunity to thoroughly try it out. Another great way to test specific models is to rent that model for a day or two.

In addition to normal items such as handling, braking, and acceleration consider the environment of the car: is the seat comfortable? Does it have enough support? Are all the controls logically placed and easily reachable? Would I feel good spending more than a few hours in the car? How well do the heater and air conditioner work? Are road and wind noise levels acceptable? What about the driving position? Am I too high or too low? Does it have a good sound system? Is there adequate interior lighting? These are just a few suggestions to think about.

You also might consider test driving a couple of other cars in the same class, even if you're not seriously considering them, to compare the car you're interested in. You may surprise yourself by finding out that the hot little number you had your heart set on really doesn't hold up well to the competition.

Bargains

Sometimes, especially if you're willing to delay gratification and perhaps settle for a car that is not your first choice, you can save thousands of dollars on a new car purchase. One way to save money is to go to a dealer at the end of a model year. Many times dealers are looking to clear out last year's models, and you can get spectacular savings — sometimes as much as $5,000 or more.

These good deals usually occur in the fall when the new models have arrived and they need to sell off old inventory. We got our minivan this way. We had saved enough for a used van and went to see one that a dealer was selling. The dealership next door had an incredibly low sale price for a minivan painted on their window. We dropped by to see how we could get this price. After finding out that the price was after rebates and student discounts (which we didn't qualify for) we were going to leave. They asked us what we could afford, and we told them the total we had, plus our old car as a trade in. This amounted to $5000 less than their sticker price of the plainest model that they sold. We left knowing that we could never afford a new car. They called us for 3 days, lowering the price each time. They couldn't lower the price of the car any more, so they started inflating the value of our trade in. It was worth about $500, but they finally gave us $3500 in credit for it. They finally got the whole package deal to within $50 of what we had saved. We stuck to our guns, stayed with the bottom line (total value, not monthly payments), and bought what we never dreamed we could own.

Other slow periods that can afford savings are in December. Most people are spending their money on other things that month. January is also slow as people reevaluate their budgets. Early April and May are good times for deals as people are using their money for tax payments, and not cars. A good basic tip to know when it is a good time to shop is if the showroom is empty. If it is, they are hungry for a deal.

If you can't wait that long to buy a car, you also can try shopping at the end of any month. Many dealers have monthly quotas, and if they haven't met them yet, they are more willing to sell at a low profit. Often, manufacturers will offer big cash rebates or financing incentives on slow-moving models. Sometimes the entire industry goes through a slump, and you can get the exact car you want at a bargain price.

Another way to get a good deal is to watch the dealer advertisements in the newspaper. To lure customers in, they offer one or two plain vehicles at a low price. They hope that you will come in and want a fancier model. The law requires them to print the vehicle ID number in the ad so that no bait and switch is taking place. We saw a Toyota pick up truck offered at $1500 below normal cost. We called the day the ad appeared to verify that the truck was still there. We were there by dinner time. We had no time to access our savings account, so we took their financing and paid it off the next month.

Haggle-Free Car Buying

Some new car dealerships have gone to haggle-free selling. Saturn pioneered this approach, but now a similar one-price-sticker approach for new cars is on the scene. AutoNation USA is a nationwide chain of dealerships, based in Fort Lauderdale, Florida, created in 1995 by Wayne Huizinga, founder of Blockbuster Video stores. Like Saturn, each car has a non-negotiable price.

There also are companies that will actually buy your car for you. These are called car-buying services. What they do is arrange for you to purchase the car of your choice through them. Usually the price you pay is only a few hundred dollars over dealer's invoice, plus fees to ship the car to a local dealership or directly to your home. Sometimes you can make an arrangement to pick up the car at the headquarters of the buying service. One such service is the Nationwide Auto Brokers (800-521-7257 or *http://www.carconnect.com)*.

Buying a Used Car

If buying a new car is too much of a hassle, or you don't have the money for a new car, try a used car. After all, even if you can avoid the salesman's traps, your new car will lose about one-fourth its value the moment you drive it off the lot. But buying a used car can present an entirely different set of hazards. The main difficulty, of course, is that unless you know the complete history of the used car you're interested in buying, you may simply be acquiring a whole set of problems from the previous owner. The car may have been in an accident that is not easily detectable, but that negatively affects the car's performance, safety, and durability. It may be a lemon. Its warranty may be nearly expired, or expired.

One way around these potential problems is to ask if you can have the car for long enough to have it thoroughly inspected by a mechanic. You may have to spend a few dollars to have this done, but you could save yourself a big headache later. My mechanic charges $100 for this service.

Research the car and model's history. Some years were filled with safety and mechanical problems for certain models and should be avoided. For example, when we wanted to buy a used Plymouth Voyager (or Dodge Caravan) we found there were a few years that were very bad for car owners. After that, they were better buys. Research the model you like at the library. Ask the reference librarian for the Consumer Digest Car Buying Guide and the Consumer Reports annual car buying issue. These also will list the annual maintenance cost for each type of car. Call the National Highway Traffic Safety Administration (NHTSA) to see if that model has ever had any recalls for safety defects (800-424-9393).

Another thing to remember when thinking about buying a used car is that finance rates are often higher for used cars than new cars — sometimes as much as two or three percentage points. Also, you may not be able to get financing for as many months on a used car. Of course, if you buy a used car from a private party, you either will need to pay cash or have financing set up in advance.

If you are buying your used car from a dealer, remember their main emphasis is getting that car looking as good as possible. Most car dealerships have detailing departments that specialize in making cars look new. Although this can result in a dazzling appearance, most of it is cosmetic, and has little or nothing to do with making the car run better. And always make sure the purchase price checks out with values of comparable vehicles in the Kelly Blue Book.

Inspect the tires for uneven wear which could indicate alignment problems. If the car has power steering, turn the steering wheel all of the way to the left and right and listen for screeches which indicate a worn belt or power steering pump. Check under the car for leaks. Test drive on a bumpy road and listen for rattles or vibrations and other noises. Test the brakes, making sure they don't screech or pull the car to one side.

Other things to check:

- *badly worn pedals or newly replaced pedals are a sign of heavily used brakes and clutch; it shows that other parts of the car have been heavily used as well*
- *windshield wiper scratches, tears in upholstery or carpet, and badly worn tires show a general neglect from the owner; if they neglected those area, the rest of the car was probably neglected as well*
- *look for oil change stickers on the door jam—if they are missing, proper maintenance may have been neglected*

- *check for repair work done—extensive body work can be indicated by ripples, bumps, or waves in the body and slight discoloration in the paint*

  (This may not rule out a car, but you need to know how sound the frame and structure are. We had a Honda that was demolished both from the rear and front, bending the frame. It was unrepairable, according to our insurance company. Several months later, we learned the car had been sold to a lady, unaware of its accident history. She had an unsafe car.)

- *mold or discoloration around window and on the carpeting; the window seals may leak*
- *check the oil dip stick; white oil or bubbles indicates expensive repairs*
- *turn the steering wheel while parked; too much play (more than two inches) indicates repairs are needed*

One way to reduce the hassle of buying a used car is to go through one of the used car superstore chains, such as AutoNation USA or CarMax. These companies feature non-commissioned sales teams and haggle-free pricing, much like Saturn. The cars have been thoroughly inspected with fluids and filters changed, worn parts replaced, and minor damages repaired. They have one-to-three month warranties, and can be returned for a full refund within five to seven days. There are hundreds of these dealerships within the AutoNation USA chain, all across the nation.

Also consider buying a used car from a rental car agency. As usual, there is an upside and a downside to this approach. The upside is that you will get a car that has been adequately maintained; it likely will have no major mechanical problems. The downside is that many people who rent cars are rather rough on them. Also, these cars tend to have higher mileage than other used cars, and it is not as easy to get a good deal.

Using the Internet

If you are online, the Internet can be a useful tool in helping make a car buying decision, either for a new or used car. There are a number of sites that will give you helpful information. You can find out such things as dealer invoices, what the actual cost of accessory packages is to dealers, reviews of cars, rankings of cars in various categories according to size and class, handling characteristics, resale values, price ranges for used cars according to mileage and condition, and many other things.

Internet Car Buying

AUTO-BY-TEL
http://www.autobytel.com
gets offers from local dealers

AUTOPRICING
http://www.autopricing.com
dealer invoice on most models

AUTO WEB
http://www.autoweb.com/info.htm
new and used cars; lists for sale by make and model

CARPOINT
http://www.carpoint.com
displays all options for a car and adds up the MSRP for you

DEALER NET
http://www.dealernet.com/
new and used cars; search by model, photos and specs

TRADER
http://www.traderonline.com
listing of used cars

KELLEY
http://www.kbb.com/
lists all current values on new and used Blue Book cars

EDMUNDS
http://www.edmunds.com/
total car shopping advice: reviews new cars for safety, road test info, dealer invoices, advice for negotiating (also available in book form at libraries & stores)

CA DEPT. OF CONSUMER AFFAIRS
http://www.smogcheck.ca.gov/CPO/100016.htm
tips for buying a used car: road test, negotiating, checklist

BLACK BOOK OFFICIAL NEW CAR INVOICE GUIDE
complete auto invoices on new cars (available at libraries & stores)

Cost of Repairs vs. Frequency of Repairs

Before you make a final decision about buying a car, you may want to look into the issue of cost of repairs vs. frequency of repairs. These may sound like the same thing, but they're actually different. Cost of repairs means how much you will have to pay to have your car repaired. Generally speaking, the more expensive the car, the more it costs for any particular repair. This is because higher priced cars often have more sophisticated parts and engineering.

Frequency of repairs means how often your car will have to be in the shop to be fixed. Generally speaking, less expensive cars will have more frequent repairs, although the cost of any single repair might be less. Thus, cost of repairs vs. frequency of repairs is often a trade off. And in many cases, you may actually end up spending less money on repairs for a more expensive car. In any case, it is wise to consult one of the consumer magazine guides, such as Consumer Reports, for repair and maintenance figures to see which cars have the best track records.

Getting the History On A Used Car

To investigate the history of a used car, all you need is the VIN (vehicle identification number) of the car. This is found on the dashboard of the car. With this, you can find if the car has been in a bad accident in the past, or if the title to the car is really owned by the person selling it to you. You can get a VIN report online through *www.edmunds.com* or *www.carprices.com,* or *www.autoweb.com.* There is usually a $12.50 fee for the service.

Safety

Tremendous advances in safety have been made in the automobile industry in the past few decades. Such things as side impact panels, air bags, seat belts and shoulder harnesses, antilock braking systems, and radial tires were unheard of 50 years ago. Nevertheless, no car traveling at high speed on the highway—no matter how many safety features it has and how well built it is—is a completely safe environment. If you have a head-on collision on the interstate with another car, and both cars are going 55 MPH, it is like hitting a brick wall at 110 miles per hour.

Once again, in the area of safety, there are trade offs. For example, the better a car handles, the greater chance you might have to avoid a collision. Yet often the cars that handle best—sports cars—are the least safe if an accident occurs. Sport utility vehicles are some of the most ruggedly built cars, often on truck platforms, but they typically do not handle very well.

CHAPTER TEN

Making Your Car Last Car Maintenance

The part of the car that causes the most accidents is the nut that holds the steering wheel.

—Anonymous

One of the biggest budget busters is car repairs. And yet, in order to get full value from your car, it is essential that you maintain it properly. Since repairs are bound to happen to every car owner, all you can do is be prepared for when it happens. One way to prepare is to create a savings account in which you contribute monthly for this impending expense. Car owners spend $70 million dollars each year on auto maintenance. That means that the average American is spending $500 per year on his own car's repairs. This is easy to imagine since the average car repair shop price runs $75 per hour. Another way to prepare is to become knowledgeable about cars and how they work.

The leading causes of breakdowns are running out of gas, cooling system problems, and tire problems. Most of these can be avoided by preventative maintenance. By periodically checking for proper coolant levels, inspecting tires for uneven wear or cracking, and keeping gas tanks filled, we would have fewer car problems.

To check your coolant levels, look under the hood for your water reservoir. Make sure it is full. If not, add coolant. Coolant can be purchased at most quick stop stores located at gas stations, Wal-Mart, K-Mart, and most auto part stores.

Changing your oil and oil filter are rather simple as well. For an excellent explanation of how to change the oil yourself, read the detailed description in *Women Home Alone* by Patricia Sprinkle, 1996, (p. 213). Here is a brief checklist of safety tips that you should keep in mind before beginning:

- *make sure you know the proper disposal of waste oil in your city (cal the city for details)*
- *avoid prolonged contact of the oil with the skin*
- *don't use thinners or gasoline to clean off the oil*
- *use waterless hand cleaners for washing hands*

Regular Maintenance

Regular car maintenance checks are like brushing and flossing your teeth. Those extra steps prevent wear that causes breakdowns. Don't rely on the indicator light on the dashboard to tell you when something is wrong and needs repair. If that light goes on, damage has already started. Here is a basic checklist of items to check on your car, and how often to check them. Some of these recommendations may differ from what you have heard in the past. These are based on recommendations of several mechanics who feel the "typical" suggestions are not needed.

Car Maintenance Checklist

Item	*Frequency*
Engine oil levels	*once per month*
Engine oil change	*5000 miles**
Engine oil filter replace	*each oil change*
Check power steering fluid	*once per month*
Check brake fluid levels	*once per month*
Spark plug replacement	*30,000 miles*
Timing belt replacement	*60,000-90,000 miles*
Air filter replacement	*15,000 miles*
Check tire pressure	*once per month*
Check tire wear	*once per month*
Check battery contacts	*once per month*

Item	*Frequency*
Check coolant levels	*once per month*
Brake pad replacement	*if pad is 1/16th or less thick*
Replace brake fluid	*when replace brake pads*
Hose replacement	*50,000-100,000 miles*
Shocks and struts replacement	*100,000 miles or more***
Coolant flush	*every other year*
Air conditioner maintenance	*only if there is a problem*

** The standard recommendation of every 3000 miles is for heavily used vehicles such as taxis, trucks, etc., not light to moderately used vehicles.*

***If someone says you need new struts, do the bounce test to see if they are right. Push down on the corner of the car that "needs new struts" and release. If the car bounces 2-3 times, that's okay. If it bounces longer, it needs new struts.*

Another thing to remember, especially if you plan on keeping your car a long time, is to have it washed regularly. This is especially important in areas that have harsh winters where salt is put on road surfaces. Since salt has a corrosive effect on metal, you should wash your car often in the winter, even if it is just going to get dirty right away again. Remember, it is much easier to fix an engine than to repair a car that has rust all over it.

Buying New Tires

I hate it when it's time for new tires. It is an expense that drains most of my car maintenance fund, and it's a pain to do. There are some better ways to buy tires other than going to the local tire dealer or car repair center. Before you buy, check out tires by mail order. Their prices are usually 35% less than retail. Even with the added expenses of shipping costs, mounting and balancing fees, and the disposal of the old tires, their cost still often comes out ahead.

Here are some tire mail order retailers:

Bell Tire Distributors..*313-271-9400*

Teletire..*800-835-8473*
(in California)..*714-250-8355*

TIRE RACK 800-428-8355

FASTIRE 800-327-8473
(in Ohio) 800-522-8472

Tire Safety Kit

Since tires are one of the main causes of roadside emergencies, having some handy tools to prevent the mishap is a good idea. The tire industry has put a kit together that may help you.

For $4, you can get a kit containing:
a pressure gauge
a tread depth gauge
4 tire valve caps
a consumer tire guide

To get this kit, send a check to:

TIRE INDUSTRY
Safety Council
Box 1801
Washington, DC 20013

Gasoline

I have had more conversations about what type of gas is best, what is needed, and what should be avoided. And each discussion ends with a different conclusion. So, after doing some additional research, I have concluded the following things about gasoline:

- *High octane is a waste of money. You only need it if you are knocking or pinging. Most cars are designed to work on low octane.*
- *The average car uses 17% less gas at 55 MPH than at 65 MPH.*
- *Fuel additives are not necessary. They don't improve the performance of your car, and can cause problems for some cars.*
- *Don't over-fill the gas tank. The gas needs some space for the vapor. If you top off the tank, you can cause damage by not leaving that space.*
- *Driving in low gear when a higher gear is available will use up to twice the amount of gas.*

- *Under-inflated tires can use up to 15% more gasoline.*
- *Fast acceleration will use excess gas.*
- *Revving the engine uses excess gas.*
- *Idling for longer than one minute wastes fuel. Turning off the car and restarting is less damaging than continuing to idle. Car idling can run up the gas bill up to $90 per year for some cars.*
- *The type of road you drive effects gas mileage: potholes use up 15% more gas than paved roads, and loose gravel roads use up 35% more gas than paved roads.*
- *Don't downshift instead of braking. It is cheaper to replace brakes than a transmission.*

WHEN YOU NEED HELP

Chances are you will need someone else to repair your car some time. Even those who tinker with their cars will need another mechanic under the hood at some time. Knowing how to spot a good mechanic is key to avoiding a rip-off. Ask for recommendations from friends. Why do they use that person? The next section will often help with that area. Even when a good mechanic is in your employ, there are some things that can help make the whole transaction smoother.

- *Be specific with your needs. Tell the mechanic in detail what the problem is and what you want repaired.*
- *When you get an estimate, don't feel pressured into agreeing to the work right away. Discuss it over with your spouse, or check your bank account first. Whatever excuse you give, use that time to research what others would charge for the same work. You'll be amazed at the variety of fees.*
- *Read about that specific area of service. See if you think the mechanic's plan sounds reasonable. There are several books at the library that discuss each area of the car and what is reasonable or not. See the Resources section in the back of this book for a listing.*
- *If you have trouble with the service received on your car, assert your rights. Explain what you wanted and what actually happened. If you cannot resolve it directly, contact the Consumer Protection Section of the Office of The Attorney General in your state capital.*

How to Spot a Good Mechanic

A government study claims that 32¢ out of every dollar spent on car repairs was for unnecessary work. You don't need to know how to fix a car to know when a repair is needed or not. But there are some ways to avoid the traps and pitfalls of bad mechanics.

The first thing to do is arm yourself with knowledge. Know some of the basics of how cars work. One example of how knowledge can help in a common trap is when you are told that your brakes need replacing. Find out what percentage is left on the brakes and read in your owner's manual what the recommended level for replacement is. Or call a dealer that sells your make of car and ask what they recommend.

Mechanic Helpline

If you wonder if your mechanic is giving you good advice, and you have no one to ask, there is a source. America's Mechanic Trustline was set up so that you can ask what a fair fee is for a job, and if the diagnosis sounds right given the symptoms. Each person you reach is a certified mechanic with at least 10 years experience.

To call, you must have the vehicle ID number (not the license plate), vehicle make, model, year and mileage. The call costs $9.95 but there is no charge if they cannot help you.

America's Mechanic Trustline.................................800-818-4191

Other ways to become knowledgeable about cars are to take a community college course on basic auto repair, read your owner's manual, read some introductory books on car repair written for the novice (there are a few recommended in the back of this book), or have a mechanic friend explain a few things to you.

Chances are pretty good that you will find good mechanics at most car repair facilities. To make sure, check for a rating of some type, such as a AAA sign. Call the Better Business Bureau to check up on them. Finally, to help you identify those that are good, here are some helpful tips.

A BAD MECHANIC MIGHT:	A GOOD MECHANIC WILL:
object to your questions	*give you a written estimate*
be rude if you suggest a solution	*give you a copy of the detailed estimate*
charge you to examine the car	*guarantee their work*
be more common on interstate highways (few people come back to complain)	

Car Repair Show

Do you wish you knew more about how your car ran, or what the news is on the latest models of car? For these and other useful tips for the car owner, tune into a national radio talk show every Saturday. Car Repair Show is live and takes callers (888-8CARSHOW) for 2 hours from 9-11 AM (EST). For more information, check out their website: *http://www.the-carshow.com/*

Final Tips

Keep a log book in the glove compartment of your car. Write down all types of service that you have done on the car. You won't be able to remember everything that you do. A log is helpful when selling the car since you can prove the care that you took. Keeping track of gas mileage in the log is also helpful. When you see the mileage dropping, have the car inspected to determine why. It may indicate a problem.

When owners of cars that had at least 150,000 miles on them were asked what they did to preserve the life of the car, they all had the following items in common:

- *changed the oil and oil filters regularly*
- *took care of minor repairs in timely manner*
- *followed the manufacturer's recommended service schedule*

Happy motoring!

CHAPTER ELEVEN

Computers For The Technologically Challenged

Home computers are being called upon to perform many new functions, including the consumption of homework formerly eaten by the dog.

–Doug Larson

HAVING ENTERED THE INFORMATION AGE, we are being drawn more and more into the high tech world of computers. Despite the trend, some people are content to remain without those time consuming machines. I recall fighting the first one we received, but since it was free from my employer (Apple Computer), I could hardly say no. There are times that I wish I had said no, but I also appreciate all that it does for us. I sometimes refer to myself as a "computer widow" since my husband spends hour after hour with it.

On the brighter side, I do enjoy the ease and speed at which a computer provides information. I couldn't have written this book without it (even though it breaks down right when I need it). I love the information that is available to me on the Internet, and how I can keep in touch via e-mail with my family and friends.

So how do we afford these beasts in our home? I am no expert, but I am frugal, so I will share what I learned from buying ours through the years.

Computers can be bought for as little as $50, or as much as several thousand dollars, with all prices in between. The difference between the cheap versions and the expensive is speed, memory, operating system features, graphics, sound, and technical support. The cheaper models will be older and may have little or no support from the manufacturer (if they are still in business). They also will not be able to support most software applications. But they are good for some very basic word processing and e-mail use.

Before choosing the features available to you, there are four things you need to know:

1. Know what your needs are.

Is the system mainly for games, e-mail, or writing reports? The type of system you get depends greatly on what you will use it for. Be honest, too. If it's mainly for games, say so. It does no good to buy a system that is mainly for word processing, and you frustratingly try and run games on it. It will stall and sputter because you lack the right stuff in it.

2. Read!

Know something about computers before you buy. Read books such as *PC for Dummies* or *Computing For Cheapskates*, or any other literature written for the beginner. Being educated will save you from making costly mistakes.

When I worked at Apple, I was responsible for buying the semiconductors that ran the Macintosh. My boss required that I give a presentation to the entire department, educating them on the workings of each device. He did this so that I was forced to learn about what I was buying. It would make me a better consumer, and able to understand anything that may come up regarding these items.

3. Buy as much as you can afford.

This may sound paradoxical coming from a miserly mom, but in the computer world I believe it is good advice. You will outgrow what you buy very quickly. The memory will fill up faster than you think it could, the RAM (see section on Memory for definition) will be too small to run the games that get released in 6 months, and the operating system won't be able to handle the applications next year.

4. Don't wait too long.

Another "strange" piece of advice from me. I say this to those who respond to point #3 by saying that they'll wait for the next level of computer to come out, and then buy. Well, you'll be waiting a long time. Every six months, new and improved models come on the market. You will never be "at the top" of the technology. Just jump in when you need one.

BUYING TIP

Computers tend to be cheaper in the early summer. New models are revealed at the Comdex personal computer convention, which is held in the spring. As the new ones arrive in the stores, last year's models tend to go on sale.

WHAT TO LOOK FOR

There are many parts to a computer system. To better understand what to buy (and avoid), here are some general overviews of the pieces.

Hard Drives

This is the storage space that will hold your files and software. It's like a filing cabinet for your stuff. And, just like a filing cabinet, the more space you have, the easier it is to get to what you need. If it's crowded and cramped, things will fall out and may even get lost or damaged. Computer data is measured in bytes (the most basic unit), megabytes or MB (1 million bytes), and gigabytes or GB (1 billion bytes). There are higher numbers but you shouldn't be needing that amount of data storage. Buy more than you need, if you can. The most frequent complaint of computer owners is that they ran out of memory.

Other features you may want built into the computer are expansion slots. These are internal slots that allow you to expand the capabilities of your computer instead of having to buy a new one when its features have become obsolete. Slots can be used for extra memory cards, sound cards, fax-modem features, and special graphics.

RECOMMENDATIONS:
1 GB (for basic word processing needs)
2 GB (if using lots of games and software)

CPU/Processor

CPU stand for Central Processing Unit. It is the brain of your computer. It decides what things to open and close, and gives all of the directions. This determines how quickly a computer program will run. It runs at a speed that is measured in megahertz (MHz). The more megahertz you have, the faster everything will run. When someone asks you how fast your system is, this is what they are referring to. If you have a fast CPU, you will need a larger amount of memory. For example, a 233 MHz processor will require a 4 GB hard drive or it will drag down the performance of your system. Look at the applications and modem speed that you plan to own, then decide on the speed of your processor.

RECOMMENDATIONS:
166 MHz (word processing, basic use of the Internet)
200 MHz (high tech games)

MANUFACTURERS THAT NEEDED THE MOST SERVICE*

1.	*Gateway 2000*
2.	*Dell*
3.	*AST*
4.	*Packard Bell*
5.	*IBM*
6.	*Compaq*
7.	*Apple*

**Consumer Reports, Sept. 97, p. 27*

Memory

The memory that I am talking about here is called RAM (random access memory). This memory is not to be confused with the memory of the hard drive. This memory is used to run the operating system. Your operating system is the system that your computer is based on (such as DOS, Windows or Mac) which oversees the operating of your programs. The more RAM you have, the faster things will run. If you have too little RAM memory, programs will freeze up while running.

RECOMMENDATIONS:
16 MB, or as much as you can afford

*Overall Satisfaction Ratings**

Apple	*91%*
Dell	*89%*
Gateway 2000	*88%*
IBM	*86%*
Compaq	*86%*
AST	*82%*
Packard Bell	*79%*

**Consumer Reports, Sept. 97, p. 27*

CD-ROM Drive

This is needed for most new software. They come in various speeds which are referred to as 4x, 6x, 8x, 16x, or 24x. You can upgrade this later, so getting the minimum is ok.

Recommendations:
8x

Monitor

The quality of the picture on your screen is determined by the space between the dots. The less space, the sharper the picture. That space is called dot pitch.

The size of the screen is for ease of use. If you use it often, such as for work, a larger screen will save you time (since more information can be displayed). If you buy a bigger screen, make sure your desk is deep enough to handle it. Anything more than 15 inches is considered deep.

Color is nice for the games and Internet, but is purely an option. The prices are very competitive these days, so color isn't much more than black and white.

Recommendations:
.28 dot pitch and 15 inches

Modem

To get your e-mail or surf the net, you will need a modem. Modem stands for MOdualte DEModulate. Modems are measured by the speed at which they transmit data. That speed is call Kbps (kilobits per second). The faster the Kbps, the quicker you get your information, and the less time you pay for using the Internet provider.

RECOMMENDATIONS:
33.6 Kbps or faster

Printer

Printers come in all styles and sizes. There is the old dot matrix type, which prints a series of dots along the paper, using a ribbon much like a typewriter. There is the ink-jet which injects ink into the paper, and then the laser printer which heats the toner drum and imprints a picture that is rolled onto paper.

If you are printing large volumes of paper, you are better off with a laser printer. They are more expensive, but worth it for those needs. These can use regular sheets of paper, but do require toner cartridge replacement once in awhile. The ink-jet printer is cheaper than the laser, has a high quality, but requires special paper so the ink won't smear. It is also slower in printing than the laser printer. Dot matrix is the slowest of all, requires special paper, is noisy, and has poor quality.

RECOMMENDATION:
whatever your need dictates

PRINTER SUPPLIES COST COMPARISON

1 ream copy paper (used for laser printers)	*$3.99*
1 ream inkjet paper	*$4.99-10.99*
toner cartridge (for laser printers)	*$99 (usage:1-2 per year)*
inkjet cartridges	*$28.99-49.99 (usage: 3-4 per year)*

Laser Cartridges

Replacing the toner cartridge in your laser printer can add up. The retail cost is around $99. We always have tried to find companies that recycle the cartridge. These companies usually give you a 50% discount by returning the cartridge and refilling it. We have never had trouble with this plan. If, however, you are doing mainly graphics printing, as opposed to text, it is not advisable to use refilled cartridges.

To find the services that refill, look in the Yellow Pages under "Computer Supplies," Office Supplies," or "Computer Printers" and ask if they refill cartridges. There is one company that refills and ships by mail order. They range from $55-85, with shipping adding only $2-$6 to the total cost. Turn around time is just a few days, and they can help with almost any model. To contact them:

AMS Laser Supply
430 S. 96th #9
Seattle, WA 98108
(800) 289-5277

Mac or PC?

This is a hard opinion for me to render. I have been a die hard Apple lover for 11 years, flaming PC users along the way. But it is my turn to eat humble pie. Having owned Macintoshes since 1987, repairing and upgrading along the way, we had to look at the cost effectiveness of doing this anymore. Our current Mac is 9 years old (an antique in computer years), and could not be upgraded any further. The decision of staying with Mac or leaving for the PC world was pressed upon us.

More and more kids' software was going the way of the PC, and the future of Apple was uncertain at the time of our decision. So, we said good-bye to Apple and became PC-ites. I didn't even feel the need to join the Appleaholics Anonymous club that exists, since I had already accepted the first of their beliefs, "We are powerless over the PC."

When to Upgrade or Buy New

- *if the computer is dragging, you may be able to just upgrade the RAM*
- *if it is seriously dragging, you can upgrade the CPU*
- *if your repairs will cost you more than $500, a new system may be needed*

What are your needs?

As I mentioned earlier, waiting for the next best system will be an endless wait, as new ones are arriving all the time. List what you primarily use the system for, and start shopping around for that need.

Here is a summary of what you may need in hardware for the type of use it will get. Remember, these are just suggestions, not absolutes. Buy what you need and can afford.

Kids

Educational software needs speed and memory to run the multimedia formats plus the sound and graphics. If you don't have these and you try and run the programs anyway, they will stall, sputter and eventually freeze up on you. This makes them unattractive to the kids, and they won't use them.

Some computer manufacturers cater to the kid market and bundle small systems for this purpose. They are small so they can fit in a kids room. I wouldn't take advantage of these since they are not upgradeable and tend to be expensive. Remember that the kids will grow up and need to do reports with graphics that will require the use of the Internet.

Recommendations:
150 MHz CPU (or faster)
24 MB memory (or faster)
2 GB hard drive memory
16x CD-ROM drive

Serious Games

If you will be using the system primarily for high tech games, your needs will be different than for kids' games. You will need faster processing, better graphics, great sound and some major memory. Avoid the business systems that are sold as packages. Stick to a personal computer package.

Recommendations:
16x CD-ROM drive (or faster)
32 MB memory (or more)
3 GB hard drive space (or more)
video cards with 4 MB memory
200 MHz CPU (or faster)

Home Business

Since time is money when running a business, you will need speed. You will also need the latest software (which keeps changing), so you will need an upgradeable system with expansion slots.

RECOMMENDATIONS:

200 MHz CPU
2 GB hard drive space
8x CD-ROM drive
video card
32 MB memory

Knowing which system to buy and who has better options can be confusing. There is a website called Computer Shopper/Net Buyer that offers easy access to information on systems made by all computer manufacturers. You can create charts online that compare features of each. You can even order directly with the manufacturer through this site. To check this service, dial them up at *http://www.zdnet.com/netbuyer*

Where to Buy

There are many ways to buy a computer these days, and all are fairly reputable. There are department stores, chain stores, small private stores, warehouse clubs, mail order and the Internet.

Chain Stores

UPSIDE:

They buy in volume, so discounts are good
They have a good selection to look at
They have good sales

DOWNSIDE:

There is no personal service or advice

Small Private Stores

UPSIDE:

Personal service
Good support

DOWNSIDE:

Less selection
Higher prices

Mail Order

UPSIDE:

Great for those who know what they want
No overhead, so low prices
Good selection

DOWNSIDE:

Waiting for delivery
Service requires finding a local support center

Internet

UPSIDE:

Great for those who know what they want
No overhead, so low prices
Good selection

DOWNSIDE:

Waiting for delivery
Service requires finding a local support center

Mail Order and Internet Computer Hardware Retailers

COMPANY	PC OR MAC	PHONE NUMBER	INTERNET ADDRESS
New MMI Corporation	*PC*	*800-221-4283*	*www.newmmi.com*
Computer Discount Warehouse	*PC/Mac*	*800-934-4239*	*www.cdw.com*
Micro Warehouse	*PC*	*800-367-7080*	*www.warehouse.com*
Mac Warehouse	*PC/Mac*	*800-434-3035*	*www.warehouse.com*
Mac/PC Connection	*PC/Mac*	*800-243-8088*	*www.pcconnection.com*
Midwest Computer Works	*PC*	*800-669-5208*	*www.mcworks.com*
The Mac Zone	*PC/Mac*	*800-248-0800*	*www.zones.com*
Computer Express	*PC*	*800-735-8700*	*www.cexpress.com*
Mac Mall	*Mac*	*800-217-9492*	*www.macmall.com*
ClubMac	*Mac*	*800-260-8549*	*www.club-mac.com*
Surplus Direct	*PC*	*800-753-7877*	*www.surplusdirect.com*

REPAIRING YOUR COMPUTER

Repairing a computer can be very costly. When you think you need repairs, first check items such as loose plugs or removing a faulty application that was newly installed. If this isn't the cause, then keep these things in mind while shopping for a service center.

- *check the Better Business Bureau for any complaints registered*
- *ask friends who they use and like*
- *check at chain retailers for a service center*
- *ask if they are an authorized service center for that manufacturer*
- *compare prices (we got quotes from $99-$299 for the same item!)*
- *consider mailing it to a repair center*

This last suggestion may sound strange, but we found that to be the best option. While living in California, we used a private repair center that was reliable, inexpensive and friendly. When our Mac broke down in Colorado, we went to the main authorized service center in town. They wanted $299 and 4 weeks to repair it. We called our service center in California, and they quoted us $99, and could return it in 10 days. We shipped the hard drive to them overnight ($28) and all went well. If you'd like to try them too, they are called All Mac (800-WE-FIX-MACS).

There are things you can do to avoid repairs to the computer. There are books with lists of things to check that can save you money. Look in the library under "computer repair" or "personal computers." Even if you can't repair a system yourself, there are things you can do to keep from damaging the sensitive components inside:

- *avoid too much heat where your computer lives*
- *avoid too much dust around the computer*
- *don't vacuum on the computer (the static can zap components)*
- *don't use any sprays around the computer (polish, solvent, hair spray, cooking sprays, cleaners, air fresheners)*
- *avoid smoking around computers as the residue settles on the components*

BUYING SOFTWARE

Getting the computer is only half of the battle. The rest is in selecting the software you need, the games you want, and then getting all of this at the cheapest price. Software can be more costly than the computer equipment, and can be habit forming, if you use your machine often.

To understand what applications to buy, I recommend talking to people about what they own. You can learn from their mistakes and successes and save yourself a lot of money. There are also many books and Internet sites that review and describe in detail software for the consumer. In addition, look at magazines for computer users such as MacWorld, PCWorld and Windows Magazine. These help us see what is available. Always make sure the software you want will be able to run on your system. Check your operating system, memory size and speed.

> FAMILY SOFTWARE REVIEWS
> *www.zdnet.com/familypc*

Once you know what you want, take your order to a discount software retailer. To beat the high price of software stores, consider mail order. They can offer lower prices since they have little overhead (warehouses require little decoration) and often can avoid sales tax, if they are out of state. These savings can often cover any shipping costs. Here is a list of mail order software companies that offer free catalogs:

Cheap Software Sources

COMPANY	PC OR MAC	PHONE NUMBER	WEBSITE
Computer Discount Warehouse	*PC/Mac*	*800-598-4CDW*	*www.cdw.com*
Micro Warehouse	*PC/Mac*	*800-367-7080*	*www.warehouse.com*
Mac Warehouse	*PC/Mac*	*800-434-3035*	*www.warehouse.com*
Mac Connection	*PC/Mac*	*800-243-8088*	*www.pcconnection.com*
PC Connection	*PC/Mac*	*800-600-9256*	*www.pcconnection.com*
Egghead Discount Software	*PC/Mac*	*800-EGG-HEAD*	*www.egghead.com*
Selective Software	*PC*	*800-423-3556*	*www.ssoftwi.com*
Surplus Direct	*PC*	*800-753-7877*	*www.surplusdirect.com*
The Mac Zone	*PC/Mac*	*800-248-0800*	*www.maczone.com*

Others can be found in the back of most computer magazines

Remnant Stores

There are also remnant software retailers who sell leftover software that may be replaced by newer designs or versions. These are a great deal, saving sometimes up to 75%.

Shareware and Free Software

Shareware is software that you can try for free, and pay a small fee if you decide to keep it. Some shareware distributors have CD-ROMS filled with shareware programs that they will mail you on a monthly basis, and you can keep and buy the ones you like. These are called shareware libraries, and they offer free catalogs.

Shareware Sources

- SHAREWARE EXPRESS 800-346-2842
- SHAREWARE EXCITEMENT 800-444-5457
- SOFTWARE LABS 800-569-7900
- MOORE ELECTRONICS 800-876-4971
- PUBLIC SOFTWARE LIBRARY 800-242-4775
- PUBLIC BRAND SOFTWARE 800-426-3475

Freeware is a program that the programmers made just for the fun of it, and give it freely for anyone to enjoy. Much of this type of software can be downloaded over the Internet.

Despite frequent rumors that shareware and freeware is riddled with viruses that will invade your hard drive, the truth is commercial software has about as many viruses as shareware and freeware. Most distributors of these items take precautions before sending them to you. If you are very nervous about this, you can buy software that searches for viruses every time you shut off or turn on your computer.

ONLINE SERVICES

Now that you have the hardware, your friends will start saying things like, "Are you on the net, yet?" "What's your e-mail address?" and other new phrases. If you dislike snail-mail as much as they do, getting on the net is something you'll want to check out.

For the more technically proficient, you will be searching for an Internet Service Provider (ISP). That is their official term. But you can use other terms such as online service or e-mail provider, and most will speak your lingo.

Many won't need to search their Internet options as their employer provides an Internet address that allows them to receive e-mail from outside of the company.

For the rest of us, searching for an ISP can be overwhelming. There are many features to consider, or perhaps ignore. You can pay a small fortune or nothing at all, depending on what you want. Here is a brief overview of some features to look for.

Type of Account

If you want to surf the net, you will want a more high tech type of account. If, however, you just want to write to Aunt Susie, a basic e-mail account will suffice.

For the high tech junkie who wants graphics on the web, you may want to ask for an SLIP/PPP type of account. Being technologically challenged myself, my explanation will be brief: an SLIP/PPP account is used for web browsing because it contains graphics. Most ISPs will know what you're talking about.

While shopping around, if you want web browser abilities, make sure that web access is included. Some ISPs are charging extra each time they allow you web access, while others have this access included. Check to see that you have the right modem speed and memory to handle the graphics that you will encounter on the web.

If all you want is an e-mail type of account, the SLIP/PPP isn't necessary. The type of account used for text only type of mail is called a shell account. There are some ISPs that only have text accounts. These are generally cheaper. There are some listed at the end of this section.

Software

Most of the ISPs are providing free software when signing on. Some, however, are still charging for this service. The major ISPs mail theirs out in magazines and advertising mailers. We have a complete collection of their free diskettes! But they are useless, unless you pay the user fees. Those vary quite a bit, as we will discuss later.

If searching for software is something you are doing, make sure to ask if it will run on your computer's operating system. I like the story of what happened to the California Department of Motor Vehicles a few years ago. They had two teams developing a new computer system to ease all of the administrative headaches of the CA DMV. One team handled the hardware while another developed the software. After millions of dollars and a few years, they were finally brought together — to find they were incompatible. The software was for another operating system. Make sure you don't make the same mistake.

As long as you are asking, make sure the ISP will have help available for installation questions and difficulties.

And if web browsing is an option you want, ask if their software will allow you to use another Internet access software, or if they require you to use theirs. Some web sites rely on ISP software such as Netscape for proper display since it has a superior web browser graphics and utilities. Other people don't want the expense of two types of software, and are happy to live within the restrictions of using only the ISP's material.

Service

There is nothing more frustrating than buying something, not having it work properly, and not being able to reach someone for help. Service is something that the ISPs must have, or their offer is not worth much. Make sure there is support at all hours, that the line is a toll-free number, and that their response time is brief. To check out this last one, call their technical support people before you buy and see how long it takes to get through. Call at peak hours like 8:00 PM on weeknights or Saturday all day.

Rates

The last thing to consider, but certainly not the least important, are the rates of an ISP. The rates vary greatly from free to several hundred dollars per year. Some charge set up fees, while others are free. Monthly rates are common, whereas others charge a per message fee. Some charge a flat rate and then add on charges when you access the worldwideweb. This is where you need to know what you want in an ISP.

If e-mail is all you want, take the free one — but make sure you know what you are getting into. The free ones get their funding from advertisements. Each time you sign on, you get loads of ads that you have to wade through before you get to the mail.

One of the free e-mail providers is Juno. They are a free e-mail service that has no set up fees, no per message charges, no monthly fees and does not require Internet access. Contact them by e-mail at info@juno.com, or on the web at *http://www.juno.com,* or toll free 800-654-5866. They also provide local phone numbers to 400 areas in the United States for signing on. If you are not in one of these calling areas, you will pay a long distance charge for each log on. This service is limited to Microsoft Windows users only (sorry Mac lovers). If web browsing is something you crave, this is not the provider for you.

There are 12 national Internet servers. Choosing among them can be confusing. Several publications have written reviews on who they think is best. I cannot list everyone's opinion here, but I have listed a few of the reviews for you. For a more thorough evaluation of each, check out these reviews (most are on the net):

Online Services and the Internet: The Network Manager's Friend or Foe? by Andy Covell
(http://www.techweb.cmp.com)

Prodigy Internet Service — a review by Shay Fulton
(http://www.mymac.com)

America Online Review
(http://www.wickedmystic.com/reviews4.htm)

The Online Deskbook
by Mary Ellen Bates, 1996 Pemberton Press

Two sites exist online that will let you find an ISP that matches your needs (area, price, computer, modem, etc.). They can be found at:

ISP Search
http://www.isps.com/advscripts/search.asp

The List
http://thelist.internet.com

PC WORLD Magazine Ratings of ISPs

These ratings were based on speed of system, response of customer service, and amount of junk mail.

1. *IBM Internet Connection*
2. *Concentric Network*
3. *Earthlink Network*
4. *MindSpring*
5. *Sprint Internet Passport*
6. *AT&T World Net*
7. *Compuserve*
8. *Prodigy*
9. *MCI Internet*
10. *Microsoft Network*
11. *Netcom*
12. *America Online*

SOURCE:
http://www.pcworld.com/workstyles/online/articles/jan98/1601p146.html

Cyber Safety For Kids

Many people are not comfortable with their kids using the Internet. Some are wary of the net due to the high volume of questionable material that pops up — and often when we are searching for something completely different. Others fear that the kids will start using chat rooms that they should avoid instead. Whatever your reason, having some ground rules for the kids' use of the computer and some added help in filtering out the junk on the web can be handy. Below are some tips on both.

Some people avoid the Internet altogether because they can't be sure what they'll run into. There is no need to let our fears keep us from the many values of the net. It can provide a wealth of information on any topic — more than you can find at your local library. For example, we have researched specific groups and clubs and we were interested in world history topics that my son is studying. It is a great tool for learning. Yes, it has its downsides (or as my husband says, "the dark side"), namely the junk and porn that shows up where it's not suppose to be. But, that's why these rules and tools were created.

Cyber Rules

Aside from the tools, there are some basic safety tips that parents can take to make the net safer. Just as we monitor what the kids watch on television, we need to be aware of what they are into on the net. Creating ground rules for the use of the computer is essential. These may be as helpful in preventing harm as teaching kids to look before crossing a street. Some of the basic safety tips they need to know in order to have the privilege of using the computer should include:

- *keep the computer in an open place where the family is—I don't recommend that a computer be put in the kids' rooms since you cannot see what is going on*
- *set hours that they are allowed to use the computer; this way you know when to be in the monitoring mode*
- *be involved and stay up on their interests; sit with them periodically while they are online so you know what they are into*
- *set a rule that the child should never give out personal information to anyone on the net, such as phone numbers, addresses or a photo—even last names should be avoided*
- *explain that people present themselves differently on the computer than they are in real life*
- *set a rule that no matter how neat the person sounds, they are to never meet anyone in person that they met on the Internet; a stranger is the same in person or on the net—it's someone you don't know and should not talk to*
- *teach them to come to a parent and tell them if anything makes them feel uncomfortable*

Have these rules written and posted near the computer.

For more information on net safety for kids, there is a great brochure by Lawrence J. Magid called, "Child Safety On The Information Highway." It is available for free by calling (800) 843-5678.

Where to Find Clean Web Sites

The following Internet sites provide links to other websites that are safe for families and kids. It is recommended that parents first check out each individual site for the appropriate content they want their kids to view.

Kid Shield / Kid Links
http://www.kidshield.com/links/index.html

Cleanweb.net / Kid Links
http://www.cleanweb.net/weblinks/kidlinks.html

Global Family Network Family Friendly Sites
http://globalfamilynetwork.com/links/

Integrity Online / Kids Stuff
http://www.integrityonline.com/kidsstuff.htm

World Village Family Site Of The Day
http://www.worldvillage.com/famsite.htm

Larry Magid's Links For Kids, Parents, And Teachers
http://www.larrysworld.com/kidslinks.html

Virtuocity Family-Friendly Sites
http://www.virtuocity.com/

Net Ministries / Christian Kids Links
http://www.netministries.org/kids.htmls

Genesis Network / For Kids Only
http://www.genesisnetwork.net/kids\index.html

K.E.W.L. Kids Excellent Web Links Great Children Sites On The Internet
http://www.cybercomm.net/~teach/

Power Online / Family And Kid Links
http://www.polnow.net/family.htm

Family Based Internet / Kids Links
http://www.safeplace.net/home/kids/kids.htm

Rated-G Online / Kidz Only
http://www.rated-g.com/Links/kidz.htm

Cyber Tools

In addition to these ground rules, the use of a software tool to help filter the junk can be helpful. These tools should never be a substitute for your care and supervision, but a helper to keep out the bad stuff. As with any tool, it isn't perfect. There are over 250 pornography websites being added to the Internet daily. It is hard to keep up with this volume and filter them all. These companies do the best that they can. Bad stuff can and will still come through. You are to be the rest of the filter.

If you choose to use a filtering tool, explain to the kids why you feel it's necessary. Also, each company that produces a filtering program uses different criteria—choose the one that fits your family values. Some filter religious cults, others sex topics, others violence, while some even consider pro-family sites offensive.

Below are some software filter programs that we looked at. Our personal favorite was CYBERsitter because they had a larger range of filter settings, and they didn't require a subscription in order to get the future filter updates — they are free:

CYBERSITTER
Solid Oak Software, Inc.
(800) 388-2761
E-mail: info@solidoak.com
Website: http://www.solidoak.com/index.html
Cost: $39
System: Windows 95

SURFWATCH
SurfWatch Software, Inc.
(800) 458-6600
E-mail: info@surfwatch.com
Website: http://www1.surfwatch.com/homes/index.html
Cost: $49
System: Mac/Windows 95

NET NANNY
Net Nanny Software International
(604) 662-8522
E-mail: netnanny@netnanny.com
Website: http://www.netnanny.com/
Cost: $27
System: Windows 95

Filtered Internet Service Providers

For more helpful information on filters for the Internet, I recommend a book by Zachary Britton called, *Safety Net—Guiding & Guarding Your Children On The Internet,* Harvest House Publishers (1998). Also look up his website at *http://www.kidshield.com*

Some Internet Service Providers (ISPs) are filtering the Internet before it reaches your computer. Most of these "clean" ISPs are not 100% effective. I recommend that you still use filtering software in addition to their service. Some of them even offer discounts to pastors, teachers and homeschoolers.

Angels Online ....(213) 876-7246
http://www.AngelsOnline.net/

CharacterLink ....(888) 330-8678
http://www.characterlink.net/

CleanWeb ....(806) 473-2700
http://www.cleanweb.net/

Covenant Promotions ....(888) 564-7555
http://www.CovenantPromotions.com/

DeoLira Telecommunication Network (DTN)....(864) 224-1900
http://www.dtnhome.com/

Family Based Internet ....(888) 535-5354
http://www.safeplace.net/home/

Family Internet ....(816) 532-6397
http://www.familyinternet.net/

FamilyConnect ....(888) 400-0434
http://www.gofamily.com/

Family Friendly Internet Access ....*(800) 800-6636*
http://ffia.net/

Family Online Network ....*(626) 792-6226*
http://www.fam.net/

INTEGRITY ONLINE ....(800) 585-6603
http://www.integrityonline.com/

MAYBERRY USA ....(504) 780-0805
http://www.mayberryusa.net/default.html

RATED-G ....(888) 711-6381
http://www.rated-g.com/

INTERSAFENET ....(877) INTERSAFE
http://www.intersafenet.com/

Navigating the net can be confusing, but it is rewarding once you get there. I have made new friends and learned oodles of things by searching some of the web browsers. There are many proficient Internet users that can help. Happy surfing!

GLOSSARY OF COMPUTER TERMS

Bytes — a basic data storage size

Megabyte (NB) — one million bytes

Gigabyte (GB) — one billion bytes

Netscape — an ISP that allows browsing of the web

Hard drives — storage space that will hold your files and software

Expansion slots — internal slots that allow you to expand the capabilities of your computer, including memory, graphics, sound, and fax modem

CPU (Central Processing Unit) — the brain of your computer, deciding what things to open and close, and gives all of the directions

Megahertz (MHz) — when someone asks you how fast your system is, this is what they are referring to

RAM (Random Access Memory) — this memory is not to be confused with the memory of the hard drive; this memory is used to run the operating system.

Operating system — system to oversee the operating of your programs (DOS, Windows or MacOS)

Modem (MOdualte DEModulate) — modems are used to transmit and receive data to and from the computer

Kbps (kilobits per second) — the speed at which modems data travels

Video card — a card inserted into the expansion slot for special monitor needs

NOTE: to look up any computer term that I have not listed, check out this web site: *http://whatis.com*

CHAPTER TWELVE

I Can't Take it Anymore! Consumer Rights

Take time to deliberate; but when the time for action arrives, stop thinking and go in.

–Andrew Jackson

IT IS VERY ANNOYING to pay for something and not have it work properly. Have you ever bought an item and it broke within a short period of time? Or perhaps it never worked properly from the beginning, but the manufacturer thinks it is working fine. Then this chapter is for you.

Consumers need to understand their rights and responsibilities before trying to resolve a problem. This knowledge will help when the other side starts to push back or resists your attempts at correcting the situation. It is also necessary to know if you are barking up the wrong tree or not. There is nothing more embarrassing than barking and complaining, only to have it pointed out that you were in the wrong all along. This scene reminds me of the old Saturday Night Live television program skit with Gilda Radner who complains and makes a public fool of herself, later having to say, "Never mind."

The Consumer's Responsibility

Every consumer is responsible for reading the instructions, reading labels, asking for advice and getting the right price. No one else can be blamed for any of these areas. When I worked at a small computer start-up company, the customer service department consisted of one person. She said that 80% of her calls came from people who didn't bother to read the directions, and wanted her to tell them what to do. Other legitimate calls could not get through as easily because the lines were jammed by those who wouldn't take responsibility for reading the directions.

Pricing is another area in which the consumer must accept responsibility. No one else can be blamed for you not getting the best price. I'm not talking about the times when an expensive item goes on sale at the same store within a few weeks of your purchase. Sometimes you can get refunded the difference in this case, since it was from the same store. I'm referring to consumers who want to return something because they found it through mail order much cheaper. That is the consumer's fault, not the retailer.

COMPLAINTS

Complaints should be based on good information. That information is a right of yours, as the consumer. You have the right to be informed of safety features, your options, and you have the right to be heard and have your complaints addressed.

In order to complain effectively, there are a few things you need to do. If you complain in person, by telephone or by mail, your approach will be slightly different in each case. But, before I go into the details of an effective complaint, I want to explain general principles.

The Art of Complaining

Complaining does not have to be a battle. Sometimes it may turn into one, but I always try and make that the last resort. I have friends who believe you have to get ugly to get anywhere. They have victorious war stories to demonstrate their point. I have a different philosophy.

Whenever I run into problems, I look at it as an opportunity for something good to happen to us. We may have to work at getting the solution we want, but we usually benefit from the mishap in some way. I call this the Silver Lining Approach. One of my favorite examples was our couch that we bought from a sofa manufacturing company. We had it manufactured for us from showroom examples, fabric samples they provided and other details from their warehouse (this was in my pre-frugal days). The couch was to be delivered in 6-8 weeks. After 9 weeks, we complained that it still wasn't ready (they ran out of fabric at the warehouse and were waiting on a shipment). For this complaint, we got free fabric protection added to the couch. After 2-3 more weeks of waiting, we called again. This time we were appeased with a superior quality mattress and springs in the fold-out sleeper inside of the couch. After a few more weeks, we were pacified with free delivery. Finally, when the couch arrived, we had a superior product, for the price of an inconvenience.

The price of inconvenience is felt differently by everyone. Some cannot tolerate the inconvenience and get very upset. Others, like myself, look at it as an opportunity for a blessing. If you expect otherwise, frustration will be with you often. If you look at it as a way to get something else, you can have some fun with it.

How To Complain

How you complain can effect the outcome. Complaining in person and politely, will usually produce the best results. When it doesn't, seeing a supervisor, writing a letter, or using a consumer advocate may be required. Try these approaches in the order they are written next time you need to tackle a consumer problem.

Complaining In Person

Most success stories in consumer rights come from those who complained in person. Clerks are sometimes intimidated by a body in front of them. However, store personnel have their own tricks to try and combat the complaining consumer. Some may try intimidation. They will try and make you feel incompetent or diminished. Others may give you the brush-off or turn the tables on you and say it's your fault. Don't react to these ploys and fall into their trap. Restate your problem and desired solution. If they persist in their attitude, go find their supervisor.

If you plan on complaining in person, do the following;

- *bring the item in the original packaging, if possible*
- *bring the sales receipt, invoice or proof of purchase (see note below)*
- *be polite*
- *try and start with the original sales person*
- *if the sales person cannot resolve the problem, go up the chain of the command*

- *clearly state the essential information such as date of purchase, what was purchased, the problem you encountered and how you want it resolved (see note below)*
- *do not be demanding*
- *document who you spoke to, the date and time and the resolution (you may need it for a future resolution)*
- *write a thank you letter to the salesperson about his/her help in how the matter was resolved*

Note on Receipts: if you no longer have the receipt or cannot find it, do not despair. Be honest with company personnel, but be persistent in the need for a solution to your problem. Remember that couch I told you about? Nine months later, the frame snapped inside one of the arms. When we bought it, we were told we had a lifetime warranty on the couch's construction, so we tried to utilize it. They originally would not help us because we could not locate the receipt or a sales number. Our name and address was no longer in their system, so we had no proof it was their couch. I continued to politely call the sales agent that currently worked there, insisting that we needed this fixed. After four months of calling, she relented, and wrote up a repair order. In this case, polite persistence paid off.

Note on Resolving: many consumers forget to decide what they want as a resolution to the problem. Make sure you think about what you want, and clearly state it at the end of your presentation of the facts. If you don't, the merchant will decide for you.

Complaining by Telephone

Sometimes complaining in person is not practical or possible, such as when you have moved away from the area or have difficulty getting around town. Telephoning, however, can be very effective if done properly. Here are some tips:

- *be polite*
- *try and talk with the original sales person*
- *if you don't know the sales person's name, or the sales person cannot resolve the problem, go up the chain of the command*
- *clearly state the essential information such as date of purchase, what was purchased, the problem you encountered and how you want it resolved (see note above)*
- *do not be demanding*

- *document who you spoke to, the date and time and the resolution (you may need it for a future resolution)*
- *write a thank you letter to the salesperson about his/her help in how the matter was resolved*

Complaining by Mail

There are times you cannot reach the company in person or by phone and have to write to them. And sometimes you have tried these other tactics only to no avail, leaving you to write to their headquarters as a last resort. If you have to take this route, keep these things in mind:

- *be patient—your issue may take a few months to get to the right person*
- *write a business format letter, including your complete address, phone number, and date*
- *avoid handwritten notes if possible*
- *include information on the item purchased, full description with model number if possible, copies of the sales receipt or proof of purchase*
- *clearly state how you want the issue resolved*
- *be polite*
- *keep copies of your letter*
- *send by certified mail, if possible; this gives you proof it was received, and requires them to respond to it*
- *if your first letter is not addressed, send a second letter, stating what you will do if this one is not addressed (see below)*

General Complaints

Sometimes a company will go "the extra mile" if they know of your unhappiness with something that happened, even if you don't have an item to exchange or return. I have written letters that explained my dissatisfaction, and the company's response was generous compensation. I wrote to United Airlines about a series of mishaps that happened with them on my last trip. None were enormous, just annoying. They responded with a $75 gift certificate. When I purchased a bag of pre-washed lettuce, it smelled musty, but looked fine. I wrote and told them about the problem, and they sent me five coupons for free lettuce.

What Do You Do Next?

If the matter is not resolved to your satisfaction after trying the above steps, then try these tips:

- *Contact your state consumer protection agency. Their number is located in your phone book under government agencies. They can help by writing to the company on your behalf, providing information on consumer law, and may help in court proceedings, if necessary.*
- *Contact the Better Business Bureau.*
- *Contact the Federal Trade Commission.*
- *Contact a consumer advocate, located at radio stations, television stations and newspapers. This can be very effective, as the companies do not want public bad press.*
- *Contact a consumer action panel. Two industries that I know of have set these up for consumers. One is for cars, the other for major appliances. If you have a problem with your item and cannot get it resolved with the retailer, try going to the panel:*

  Major Appliances Consumer Action Panel
  20 N. Wacker Circle, Suite 1550
  Chicago, ILL 60606
  (312) 984-5858

  AUTOCAP
  Automobile Trade Association
  National Capital Area Branch
  15873 Crabbs Branch Way
  Rockville, MD 20855
  (301) 670-1110

- *Call your credit card company. Some will help you resolve your problem with the manufacturer or retailer, if you used their card to purchase it.*
- *As a last resort, you can sue in small claims court or regular court, depending on the dollar value of the claim. Make sure you have followed all of the recommended steps before taking this route, and have all documentation proving all steps were taken to prevent this court claim.*

Credit Card Advantages

There are some advantages to using a credit card for some purchases. Check to see if your credit card company has any of these features.

Travel Insurance

If you die or are disabled by an accident that involves a public carrier (planes, buses, trains, ships).

Warranty Extension

Some card companies will extend the original warranty of some items. Usually items that have long original warranties.

Purchase Protection

Accidental damage or theft of a recently purchased item is sometimes covered by the card if the purchase was made with the card, and the damage takes place within a certain amount of time from the date of purchase.

NOTE: don't buy credit card insurance. These policies protect you from excessive charges in case you lose the card. They are not necessary since federal law limits your liability to $50 if you notify the card company immediately—and many companies will even waive that $50 liability if they were notified within 24 hours.

WHAT ARE YOUR RIGHTS?

The Federal Trade Commission (FTC) was established to regulate consumer transactions. It focuses on deceptive practices, false advertising, phony investment schemes and bogus health claims. It has established some rules such as the Funeral Rule (requires funeral homes to disclose all prices and information about their goods and services, and that coffins do not have to be purchased from the home to have a service or burial there), the Cooling Off Rule (gives a buyer three days to cancel a sale of $25 or more, if the sale is made other than at the seller's place of business), and the Used Car Rule (requires the dealer to post warranty and other information). Some of the rules they have established are more encompassing, as described below.

Advertising Rules

We are all familiar with ads: they get our attention and draw you into the store. Let's look at what ads can and cannot do.

- *advertising is not the same as an offer*
- *an offer is legally binding*
- *an offer must have four points: who is making the offer, the subject matter of the offer, quantity of items in the offer, and price*
- *bait-and-switch is illegal (this is where an advertised item is not available and never was); make sure you can see the advertised model and compare it to others being offered*

Mail Order and Telephone Sales Rules

This category covers anything advertised or ordered by mail, phone, fax, or computer.

- *goods must be shipped within the specified time period—if no time period was specified, then it must be mailed within 30 days of the order*
- *if the time frame cannot be met, the merchant must notify you of the delay and offer a refund if desired*
- *no substitute items have to be accepted by you*
- *unordered merchandise is to be considered a gift, and there is no obligation to pay—if a bill arrives for unordered merchandise, this is fraud*
- *paying with a credit card helps resolve disputes easier—the credit card company sometimes helps you resolve the issue*
- *to remove yourself from the National Direct Mail lists, write to DMA Mail Preference Service, P.O. Box 9008, Farmingdale, NY 11735-9008*
- *to remove yourself from telephone marketing lists, write to DMA Telephone Preference Service, P.O. Box 9014, Farmingdale, NY 11735-9014*
- *if you have a mail order matter that cannot be resolved with the recommended suggestions, try contacting these people for help; Direct Marketing Association (DMA), Suite 1100, 1111 19th Street, NW, Washington DC 20036*

Warranties

A warranty is a statement about the manufacturer's confidence in his product. The better quality products usually have a superior warranty. There are two types of warranties—expressed warranties and implied warranties.

Here's the difference:

Expressed Warranties
This is a promise to back up any warranty that is written or given orally by the seller.

Implied Warranties
These are automatic warranties, supported by law. These types of warranties imply that an item is fit for what it was sold for. For example, the shirt must be able to withstand washing. The milk carton must have milk in it that is drinkable. This warranty also assumes that an item will last for a reasonable amount of time. That time will be determined by the store manager or manufacturer.

Whatever the warranty is, you must be able to read it, the language must be plain and clear, the address of the company must be printed on it, the length of the warranty and parts covered must also be declared.

Exceptions
There are some places that you will find the implied warranty to be extremely hampered. Places like thrift stores, boutiques and consignment shops have very limited time periods for returning items, or they expect you to check the item thoroughly and take some responsibility for your choice.

If you have trouble with a warranty item, try and do the following:

- *return the item in its original shipping container (keep those boxes!)*
- *don't try to fix the item yourself—even opening the device's outer casting voids most warranties*
- *keep good records and receipts*

Note on Warranties
You do not have to return the warranty cards inside the products you purchase. These are not used to validate your warranty, but rather are used to notify you of future product upgrades or recalls.

Resources

The following section is a list of resources that we either used in our research for this book, or recommend that you research for further information on that particular subject. We hope it helps you on your journey to frugality!

BOOKS

Books On Getting Home

Burkett, Larry. *Women Leaving The Workplace—How To Make The Transition From Work To Home,* Moody Press, 1995

Burton, Linda, Dittmer, Janet, Loveless, Cheri. *What's A Smart Woman Like You Doing At Home?* Acropolis Books (revised edition), 1992

Dorn, Katie K. *From Briefcase To Diaper Bag—How I Quit My Job, Stayed Home With My Kids and Live To Tell About It,* Time Books, 1995

Field, Christine. *Coming Home To Raise Your Children—A Survival Guide For Moms,* Revell, 1995

Fox, Isabelle. *Being There: The Benefits Of A Stay-At-Home Parent,* Barron's Educational Series, 1996

Hunter, Brenda. Home *By Choice: A Decision Every Mother Must Face,* Multnomah Books, 1996

Lewis Deborah S. and Yoest, Charmaine C. *Mother In The Middle—Searching For Peace In The Mommy Wars,* Zondervan Publishing House, 1996

Otto, Donna. *The Stay At Home Mom—For Women At Home & Those Who Want To Be,* Harvest House Publishers, 1997

Sanders, Dacie and Bullen, Martha. *Staying Home: From Full-time Professional To Full-Time Parent,* Little, Brown and Company, 1992

Tolliver, Cindy, *At-Home Motherhood — Making It Work For You,* Resource Publication, 1994

Books On Frugal Living

Bredenberg, Jeff. *Beat The System—1,200 Tips For Coming Out On Top In Every Deal And Transaction,* Rodale Books, 1997

Dacyczyn, Amy. *The Tightwad Gazette, Vol I, II, III,* Villard Books, 1993,1995, 1997

Dappen, Andy. *Cheap Tricks, 100s Of Ways You Can Save 1000s Of Dollars,* Brier Books, 1992

Dappen, Andy. *Shattering The Two-Income Myth: Daily Secrets For Living Well On One Income,* Brier Books, 1997

Ellis, Gwen and Janssen, Jo Ann. *Decorating on a Shoestring,* Broadman Holman, 1999

Hamilton, Leslie. *The Cheapskate's Guide To Living Cheaper And Better,* Citadel Press, 1996

Hancock, Maxine. *Living On Less & Liking It More,* Baker Book House, 1996

Horowitz, Shel. *The Penny-Pinching Hedonist—How To Live Like Royalty With A Peasent's Pocketbook,* AWM Book, 1995

Hunt, Mary. *The Cheapskate Monthly: Debt-Proof Your Holiday,* St. Martins, 1997

Hunt, Mary. *The Complete Cheapskate: How to Break Free From Money Worries Forever, Without Sacrificing Your Quality of Life,* Focus on the Family Publishing, 1997

Hunt, Mary. *Tiptionary;* Broadman & Holman Publishers, 1997

Jurgensen, Barbara. *How To Live Better On Less,* Augsburg Publishing House, 1974

King, Dean. *The Penny Pincher's Almanac—Handbook For Frugality,* Simon and Schuster, 1992

Larsen, Dale and Sandy. *How To Spend Less & Enjoy It More,* InterVarsity Press, 1994

Levine, Karen. *Keeping Life Simple-7 Guiding Principles 500 Tops & Ideas,* Storey Publishing, 1996

McBride, Tracey. *Frugal Luxuries-Simple Pleasures To Enhance Your Life And Comfort Your Soul,* Bantam Books, 1997

McCoy, Jonni. *Miserly Moms—Living On One Income In A Two Economy,* Full Quart Press, 1996

Miller, Mark W. *The Sensible Saver, Sensible Saver Publications,* 1996

Moore, Melodie. *The Frugal Almanac,* Publications International, 1997

Paris, James, L. *Money Management For Those Who Don't Have Any,* Harvest House, 1997

Potter, Michelle A. *The Complete Saving Source Catalog—A Guide To Saving The Earth And Money,* RIMA World Press, 1996

Quinn, Hope Stanley and Miller-Lachmann, Lyn. *Downsized But Not Defeated—The Family Guide To Living On Less,* Andrews McMeel Publishing, 1997

Reid, Lisa. *Raising Kids With Just A Little Cash,* Ferguson-Carol Publishers, 1996

Roberts, William. *How To Save Money On Just About Everything,* Strebor Publications, 1993

Roth, Larry. (Editor) *The Simple Life: Thoughts On Simplicity, Frugality, And Living Well,* Berkley Press, 1998

Roth, Larry. *Beating The System: The Next American Revolution,* Living Cheap Press, 1995

Roth, Larry. *The Best Of Living Cheap News—Practical Advice On Saving Money And Living Well,* Contemporary Books, 1996

Simmons, Lee and Barbara. *Penny Pinching—How To Lower Your Everyday Expenses, Without Lowering Your Standard Of Living,* Bantam Books, 1997

Sorenson, Stephen and Amanda. *Living Smart, Spending Less,* Moody Press, 1993

Sprinkle, Patricia H. *Women Home Alone: Learning To Thrive: Help For Women, Single Moms, Widows, And Wives Who Are Frequently Alone,* Zondervan Publishing House,1996

Taylor-Hough, Debroah. *Simple Living—One Income Living In A Two Income World,* Simple Pleasures Press, 1995 (P.O. Box 941, Auburn WA 98071-0941, $5.00 ppd.)

Yates, Cynthia. *1,001 Bright Ideas To Stretch Your Dollars,* Servant Publications, 1995

Yates, Cynthia. *The Complete Guide To Creative Gift-Giving,* Servant Publications, 1997

Yorkey, Mike. *21 Days To A Thrifty Lifestyle: A Proven Plan For Beginning New Habits,* Zondervan Publishing House, 1998

Yorkey, Mike. *Saving Money Any Way You Can: How to Become a Frugal Family,* Vine Books, 1994

Books On Money and Kids

Blue, Ron and Judy. *Raising Money-Smart Kids—How To Teach Your Children The Secrets Of Earning, Saving, Investing, And Spending Wisely,* Thomas Nelson Publishers, 1992

Bodnar, Janet. *Kiplinger's Money-Smart Kids,* Kiplinger Books, 1993

Briles, Judith. *Raising Money-Wise Kids,* Northfield Publishing, 1996

Burgeson, Nancy. *Money Book for Kids,* Troll Associates, 1991

Burkett, Larry and Osborne, Rick. *Financial Parenting: Teaching Kids That Money Matters,* Chariot Victor Publishing, 1997

Godfrey, Neales S. and Edwards, Carolina. *Money Doesn't Grow On Trees: A Parent's Guide To Raising Financially Responsible Children,* Fireside Publishing, 1994

Otfinoski, Steve. *The Kid's Guide To Money: Earning It, Saving It, Spending It, Growing It, Sharing It,* Scholastic Trade, 1996

Ryan, Bernard and Lewin, Elizabeth. *Simple Ways To Help Your Kids Become Dollar-Smart: 125 Ways To Teach Children The Value Of Money,* Walker & Company, 1994

Books On Frugal Pet Care

Bowman, Linda. *Free Stuff For Your Pet,* Probus Publications, 1992

Guidry, Virginia P. *Pet Care On A Budget,* Howell Book House, 1998

Palike, Liz. *The Consumer's Guide To Cat Food-What's In Cat Food, Why It's There, And How To Choose The Best Food For Your Cat,* Macmillan, 1996

Papai, Franki. *The Cat Lover's Cookbook,* St. Martin's Press, 1993

Pitcairn, Richard. *Natural Health For Dogs And Cats,* Rodale Press, 1982

Books On Frugal Gardening

Autry, James. *Better Homes And Gardens Complete Guide To Gardening,* Meredith Corporation, 1979

Bailey, Ralph. *Good Housekeeping Basic Gardening Techniques,* Hearst Corporation, 1974

Barron, Pattie. *The First-Time Gardener,* Crown Publishing, 1996

Bartholomew, Mel. *Square Foot Gardening,* Rodale Press, 1981

Barton, Barbara J. *Gardening By Mail—A Source Book,* Mariner Books, 1997

Buchanan, Rita. *Vegetables Step-By-Step,* Better Homes And Gardens, 1997

Connor, Jane and Sweeney, Emma. *The Complete Idiot's Guide To Gardening,* Alpha Books, 1996

Garden Way. *Fruits And Vegetables: 1001 Gardening Questions Answered,* Doubleday Book And Music Club, 1990

Harrington, Geri. *Cash Crops For The Thrifty Gardener,* GD/Perigee Book, 1984

Hart, Rhonda Massingham. *Dirt Cheap Gardening-Hundreds Of Ways To Save Money In Your Garden,* A Garden Way Publishing Book, 1995

MacCaskey, Michael. *Gardening For Dummies,* IDG Books, 1996

National Gardening Association. *Gardening: The Complete Guide To Growing America's Favorite Fruits And Vegetables,* Addison-Wesley Publishing, 1986

Walls, Ian G. *Low-Cost Gardening,* Ward Lock, 1992

Books On Frugal Travel And Vacations

Hubbell, Beth. *Luxury Travel For The Unrich and Unfamous,* Jeremiah Publications, 1992

Kaye, Evelyn. *Family Travel—Terrific New Vacations For Today's Families,* Blue Penguin Publications, 1993

Kaye, Evelyn. *Free Vacations & Bargain Adventures In The USA,* Blue Penguin Publications, 1995

Ogintz, Eileen. *Are We There Yet?—A Parent's Guide To Fun Family Vacations,* HarperSanFrancisco, 1996

Sutherland, Laura and Deutsch, Valerie W. *The Best Bargain Family Vacations In The U.S.A,* St. Martin's Griffin, 1997

Tristram, Claire and Lucille. *Have Kid Will Travel—101 Survival Strategies For Vacationing With Babies And Young Children,* Andrews McMeel Publishing, 1997

Books On Getting Out Of Debt & Being Financially Free

Avanzini, John. *Rapid Debt-Reduction Strategies,* His Publishing, 1990

Blue, Ron. *Taming The Money Monster—Five Steps To Conquering Debt,* Focus On The Family Publishing, 1993

Feinberg, Andrew. *Down Size Your Debt,* Prentice Hall Press, 1993

Hammond, Bob. *Life After Debt: How To Repair Your Credit And Get Out Of Debt Once And For All,* Career, 1993

Hunt, Mary. *The Cheapskate Monthly Makeover,* St. Martin's Paperbacks, 1995

Mundis, Jerold. *How To Get Out Of Debt, Stay Out Of Debt & Live Prosperously,* Bantam Books, 1990

Thomsett, Michael C. *How To Get Out Of Debt,* Irwin Publishing, 1990

Books On Budget Planning

Burkett, Larry. *Family Budget Workbook—Gaining Control Of Your Personal Finances,* Northfield Publishing, 1993

Burkett, Larry. *Larry Burkett's Cash Organizer: Envelope Budgeting System,* 1995

Lawrence, Judy. *The Budget Kit—The Common Cents Money Management WorkBook,* Dearborn Financial Publishing, 1993

Longo, Tracey. *10 Minute Guide To Household Budgeting,* Alpha Books, 1997

McCullough, Bonnie. *Bonnie's Household Budget Book—The Essential Guide For Getting Control Of Your Money,* St. Martin's Griffin, 1996

Peetz, Tuttie. *Basic Budgeting And Money Management: A Guide For Taking Control Of Your Spending,* Systems Company, 1997

Books On Frugal Savings And Investing

Barnes, Bob and Emilie. *The 15-Minute Money Manager,* Harvest House, 1993

Blue, Ron. *Master Your Money,* Thomas Nelson Publishers, 1991

Briles, Judith. *Moneysense-What Every Women Must Know To Be Financially Confident,* Moody Press, 1995

Burkett, Larry. *The Complete Guide to Managing Your Money,* Budget Book Service, 1996

Burkett, Larry. *Your Complete Guide To Financial Security—Investing For The Future And Preparing For Retirement,* Budget Book Service, 1998

Burkett, Larry. *A Guide To Family Budgeting,* Focus on the Family, 1993

Chilton, David. *The Wealthy Barber: Everyone's Commonsense Guide to Becoming Financially Independent,* Prima Publishing, 1997

Dunnan, Nancy. *How To Invest $50-$5,000-The Small Investor's Step-By-Step, Dollar-By-Dollar Plan For Low-Risk, High-Value Investing,* Colverdale Press, 1997

Eisenson, Marc. *The Banker's Secret,* Villard Books, 1990

Eisenson, Marc, Detweiler, Gerri, and Castleman, Nancy. *Invest in Yourself: Six Secrets to a Rich Life,* Wiley & Sons, Inc., 1998

Kelly, Jason. *The Neatest Little Guide To Mutual Fund Investing,* Plume, 1996

Moore, Gary. *Ten Golden Rules For Financial Success,* Zondervan Publishing House, 1996

O'Neill, Barbara. *Saving On A Shoestring—How To Cut Expenses Reduce Debt Stash More Cash,* Berkley Books, 1995

Pond, Jonathan D. *The New Century Family Money Book—Your Comprehensive Guide To A Lifetime Of Financial Security,* DTP, 1995

Pryor, Austin. *Sound Mind Investing: A Step-By-Step Guide to Financial Stability & Growth As We Move Toward the Year 2000,* Moody Press, 1996

Scott, David. *The Guide To Saving Money,* Globe Pequot Press, 1996

Skousen, Mark. *Scrooge Investing—The Bargain Hunter's Guide To More Than 120 Things You Can Do To Cut The Cost Of Investing,* Little, Brown and Company, 1996

Steamer, James. *Wealth On Minimal Wage,* Dearborn Financial Publishing, 1997

Strohm, Richard. *Layman's Law Guide: Solving Your Financial Problems,* 1994

Tyson, Eric. *Personal Finance For Dummies,* IDG Books, 1996

Wall, Ginita. *The Way To Save: A 10-Step Blueprint For Lifetime Security,* Henry Holt and Co., 1997

Books On Frugal Savings On Medical Care

Inlander, Charles B. *150 Ways To Be A Savvy Medical Consumer,* Wings Book, 1992

Inlander, Charles B. and Morales, Karla. *Getting The Most For Your Medical Dollar,* Pantheon Books, 1991

Marshall, Howard B. *How To Save Your Teeth—The Preventive Approach,* Everest House Publishers, 1980

Nader, Ralph and Smith, Wesley J. *Winning The Insurance Game,* Doubleday, 1993

Ulene, Art. *How To Cut Your Medical Bills,* Ulysses Press, 1994

Books On Frugal Buying Or Repairing Household Appliances

Cohen, Daniel. *The Last Hundred Years: Household Technology,* M. Evans & Co., 1982

Gramm, Barbara Fairchild. *And You Think You've Got It Bad,* 1989

Kleinert, Eric. *Troubleshooting & Repairing Major Appliances,* Tab Books, 1995

Rains, Darell L. *Major Home Appliances—A Common Sense Repair Manual,* Tab Books, 1987

Schultz, Mort. *Fix It Yourself For Less,* Consumer Reports Books, 1993

Wood, Robert W. *All Thumbs Guide To Repairing Major Home Appliances,* Tab Books, 1992

Books On Frugal Savings On New & Used Home Furnishings

Causey, Kimberly. *The Insider's Guide To Buying Home Furnishings—How And Where Anyone Can Buy High-Quality Designer Brands At Wholesale Prices Without Hiring A Designer,* Home Decor Press, 1996

Books On Frugal Car Buying

Annechino, Daniel M. *How To Buy The Most Car For The Least Money: Negotiate The Lowest Possible Price For A New Car Every Time,* Nal/Dutton, 1993

Blazak, Robert M. *Carbuying 101—How To Buy A Car With The Change In Your Ashtray,* Rainbow Books, 1997

Edgerton, Jerry. *Car Shopping Made Easy: Buying Or Leasing New Or Used,* Warner Books, 1997

Elliston, Bob. *What Car Dealers Won't Tell You: The Insider's Guide To Buying Or Leasing A New Or Used Car,* Nal/Dutton, 1996

Eskeldson, Mark. *What Car Dealers Don't Want You To Know,* Technews Publishing, 1995

Haynes Editors. *The Haynes Used Car Buying Guide* (Techbook Series), Haynes Publications, 1996

Hazleton, Lesley. *Everything Women Always Wanted To Know About Cars: But Didn't Know Who To Ask,* Doubleday, 1995

Intellichoice Staff. *Complete Car Cost Guide,* 1996, Intellichoice, Inc., 1996

Kilmer, Scott M. *Everyone's Guide To Buying A Used Car And Car Maintenance,* On The Road Publishing, 1994

Leon, Burke and Stephanie. *The Insider's Guide To Buying A New Or Used Car—Hundred Of Tips In Easy-To-Use Checklist Format* From A Veteran Insider, Betterway Books, 1997

Levy, Daniel. *Automobile Aerobics, Exercise Your Right To Trim Thousands Off The Price Your Next Automobile And Make The Dealership Sweat!* Tennyson Publishing, 1996

Mateja, Jim. *Best Buys In Used Cars,* Bonus Books, 1995

Parrish, Darrell B. *Used Cars: How To Buy One,* Artesia, 1995

Parrish, Darrell. *The Car Buyer's Art—How To Beat The Salesman At His Own Game,* Book Express, 1996

Sennert, Ronald And Barbara. *How To Save $9,000 On Your Next Car Or Van,* Proud American Publishing, 1991

Stargel, Sky. *The Blue Book Of Car-Buying Secrets,* Best Cellar Books, 1993

Books On Saving Money On Car Repairs

Burgoyne, J. Robert. *You Can Cut Car Costs,* FYI, 1992

Fendell, Bob. *How To Make Your Car Last A Lifetime,* Holt, Rinehart, And Winston, 1981

Fremon, George And Suzanne. *Why Trade It In?, Keep Your Car Trouble-Free,* Liberty Publishing, 1991

Glickman Authur P. *Avoiding Auto Repair Rip-Offs,* Consumer Reports Books, 1995

Goulter, Vic And Barbara. *How To Keep Your Car Mechanic Honest,* Scarborough House, 1990

Schultz, Mort. *Keep Your Car Running Practically Forever—An Easy Guide To Routine Care And Maintenance,* Consumer Reports Books, 1991

Shumway, Jeff. *The Answer: Getting More And Paying Less For Auto Service,* Preston House, 1996

Sikorsky, Robert. *Drive It Forever, Your Key To Long Automobile Life,* Mcgraw-Hill Publishing, 1983

Sikorsky, Robert. *Rip-Off Tip-Offs-Winning The Auto Repair Game,* Tab Books, 1990

Stevenson, Chris. *Auto Repair Shams And Scams—How To Avoid Getting Ripped Off,* Price Stern Sloan, 1990

Consumer Guide Staff. *Used Car Buying Guide,* 1997, Nal/Dutton, 1997

Fariello, Sal. *The People's Car Book: The Car Book For People Who Don't Trust Mechanics,* Car Salesmen, Or Car Manufacturers, St. Martin, 1993

Magliozzi, Tom And Ray. *Car Talk,* Dell, 1991

Morton, B. A. *How Women Win The Auto Repair Game: A Consumer Survival Guide,* Carsmart Publications, 1996

Schultz, Mort (Editor). *What's Wrong With My Car?*, Consumer Reports Books, 1990

Sclar, Deanna. *Auto Repair For Dummies,* Ten Speed Press, 1989

Books On Frugal Personal Computing

Britton, Zachary. *Safety Net—Guiding & Guarding Your Children On The Internet,* Harvest House Publishers, 1998

Gookin, Dan. *PCs For Dummies,* IDG Book, 1997

Nadler, Bob. *Computing For Cheapskates,* Ziff-Davis Press, 1994

Pearson, Olen R. *Guide To Personal Computers,* Consumer Reports Books, 1996

Pearson, Olen R. *Personal Computer Buying Guide,* Consumer Reports Books, 1993

Books On Consumer Rights

American Bar Association. *Guide To Consumer Law,* Random House, 1997

Hernandez, MaryBeth. *Know Your Rights: A Guide To Consumer Protection,* Janus Book Publishers, 1984

Lieberman, Marc R. *Your Rights As A Consumer—Legal Tips For Savvy Purchases Of Goods, Services And Credit,* Chelsea House Publishers, 1994

McCohan, Donna. *Get What You Pay For Or Don't Pay At All—Consumer Resource Manual,* Crown Trade Paperbacks, 1994

Oshiro, Carl Snyder. *Getting Action: How To Petition State Government,* Consumer Union of United States, Inc., 1980

Portnoy, J. Elias. *Let The Seller Beware!—The Complete Consumer Guide To Getting Your Money's Worth,* Collier Books, 1990

Ross, Linda. *The Smart Consumer's Book Of Questions,* Chicago Review Press, 1996

Sack, Steven Mitchell. *Don't Get Taken,* Legal Strategies Publications, 1996

Singer, Arlene, and Parment, Karen. *Take It Back!—The Art Of Returning Almost Anything,* National Press Books, 1991

Books On Grocery Savings & Cooking Inexpensive Meals

Barfield, Rhonda. *Eat Healthy For $50 A Week: Feed Your Family Nutritious, Delicious Meals for Less,* Kensignton Publishing, 1996

Bond, Jill. *Dinner's In The Freezer!—More Mary And Less Martha,* Holly Hall Publications, 1993

Bond, Jill. *Mega Cooking—A Revolutionary New Plan For Quantity Cooking To Save You Time, Money, and Energy in Food Preparation,* Holly Hall Publications, 1998

Eckhardt, Linda West. *Feed Your Family On $10.00 A Day—Fast, Healthy Meals,* Peregrine Smith Books, 1993

Hunt, Mary. *Cheapskate In The Kitchen—Everything You Need To Know About Creating Fabulous Meals At A Fraction Of The Cost!,* St. Martin Press, 1997

Kaysing, Bill and Ruth. *The 99¢ A Meal Cookbook,* Loompanics Unlimited, 1996

Kaysing, Bill. *Eat Well For 99¢ A Meal,* Loompanics Unlimited, 1996

Taylor-Hough, *Debroah. Frozen Assets—How To Cook For A Day And Eat For A Month,* Champion Press, 1998

Taylor-Hough, Debroah. *Mix-N-Match Recipes,* Simple Pleasures Press, 1997 (P.O. Box 941, Auburn WA 98071-0941, $5.00 ppd.)

Books On Bargain Hunting And Yard Sales

Bamel, Jody. *Save Yourself A Fortune! The Bargain Hunter's Guide To Flea Markets, Thrift Shops Yard Sales, Actions, Antique Stores, Estate Sales And More,* Berkeley Books, 1995

Drury, Treesa. *Savvy Shopper,* J.P. Tarcher, 1974

Hoff, Al. *Thrift Store: The Stuff, The Method, The Madness,* Harper Collins, 1997

King, Trisha and Newmark, Deborah. *Buying Retail Is Stupid!* Contemporary Books, 1996

McClurg, R. S. *The Rummager's Handbook—Finding, Buying, Cleaning, Fixing, Using, And Selling Secondhand Treasures,* Storey Communications Inc., 1995

Schmeltz, L. R. *The Backyard Money Machine—How To Organize And Operate A Successful Garage Sale,* Silver Streak Publications, 1993

Schneider, Carolyn. *The Ultimate Consignment And Thrift Store Guide,* Consignment & Thrift Store Publishing, 1997

FRUGAL NEWSLETTERS DIRECTORY

LIVING CHEAP NEWS
Larry Roth, Editor
P.O. Box 8178
Kansas City, MO 64112
$12.00/yr/10 Issues
Sample issue: free w/ #10 (long) SASE
E-mail address: Livcheap@aol.com

FRUGAL TIMES
Tracey McBride, Editor
P.O. Box 5877
Garden Grove, CA 92645
$14.00/yr/4 issues
Sample issue: $1.00 w/ #10 (long) SASE

THE POCKET CHANGE INVESTOR
Marc Eisenson, Editor
P.O. Box 78, Elizaville, NY 12523
$12.95/yr/4 issues
Sample issue: $1.00
E-mail address: goodadvice@ulster.net
Website address: http://www.goodadvicepress.com

A PENNY SAVED
Diane Rosener, Editor
P.O. Box 3471
Omaha, NE 68103-0471
$14.00/yr/6 issues
Sample issue: $3.00
E-mail address: apnnysvd@juno.com

CREATIVE DOWNSCALING
Edith Kilgo, Editor
P.O. Box 1884, Dept. MM
Jonesboro, GA 30237-1884
$15.00/yr/6 issues
Sample issue: $2.00
E-mail address: kilgo@mindspring.com
Website address: http://www.mindspring.com/~kilgo/index.html

THE FRUGAL BUDGET BOOSTER
Laurie Spinney, Editor
61 Paul Street
South Berwick, ME 03908
$15.00/yr/12 issues
Sample issue: $2.00
E-mail address: kspinney@nh.ultranet.com
Website address: http://www.nh.ultranet.com/~kspinney

BIG IDEAS SMALL BUDGET
Pat Wesolowski, Editor
2201 High Road
Tallahassee, FL 32303
$12.00/yr/11 issues
Sample issue: $1.00
E-mail address: quiver_full@juno.com

CHEAPSKATE MONTHLY
Mary Hunt, Editor
P.O. Box 2135
Paramount, CA 90723-8135
$18.00/yr/12 issues
Sample issue: free by sending your name and address
E-mail address: cheapsk8@ix.netcom.com
Website address: http://www.cheapskatemonthly.com/

SAVVY DISCOUNTS NEWSLETTER
Rick Doble, Editor
P.O. Box 96
Smyrna, NC 28579
$9.95/yr/4 issues
Sample issue: free-send postcard
E-mail address: savvynews@mail.clis.com
Website address: http://www.clis.com/savvynews/

THE DOLLAR STRETCHER
Gary Foreman, Editor
P.O. Box 23785
Ft. Lauderdale, FL 33307
$18.00/yr/12 issues
Sample issue: $1.00
E-mail address: gary@stretcher.com
Website address: http://www.stretcher.com

THE FRUGAL GAZETTE
Cynthia McIntyre, Editor
P.O. Box 3395
Newtown, CT 06470-3395
$15.95/yr/12 issues
Sample issue: free w/ #10 (long) SASE
E-mail address: cindy@frugalgazette.com
Website address: http://www.frugalgazette.com/

KEEP YOUR CASH
Cindy Van Gelder, Editor
P.O. Box 2234
Holland, MI 49422-2234
$12.00/yr/12 issues
Sample issue: free w/ #10 (long) SASE

BALANCING ACT
Betsy Giese Sullivan, Editor
P.O. Box 309
Ghent, NY 12075-0309
$6.00/yr/6 issues
Sample issue: $1.00 w/#10 (long) SASE
E-mail address: balancinga@aol.com
Website address: http://members.aol.com/balancinga/ba.html

FRUGAL FAMILY NETWORK NEWSLETTER
Deana Ricks and Angie Zalewski, Editors
P.O. Box 92731
Austin, TX 78709
$10.00/yr/6 issues
Sample issue: free w/#10 (long) SASE
E-mail address: Frugal4U@frugalfamilynetwork.com
Website address: http://www.frugalfamilynetwork.com

COUNTING THE COST
Nancy Twigg, Editor
4770 Germantown Road, Extd.
Suite 122
Memphis, TN 38141
$15.00/yr/12 issues
Sample issue: $2.00
E-mail address: counting.the.cost@mailexcite.com
Website address: http://members.xoom.com/nancyT/CTChome.htm

FRUGAL ELECTRONIC NEWSLETTERS

THE SIMPLE TIMES
(subscription every two weeks)

To subscribe to this list, send a message to: *hub@XC.Org*

The subject line is unimportant. In the message body, on the very 1st line write:

subscribe simple-times

To unsubscribe to this list, you can send mail to:

hub@XC.Org

The subject line is unimportant. In the message body, on the very 1st line write:

unsubscribe simple-times

If you need further assistance regarding the Simple-Times contact:

owner-simple-times@XC.Org

THE DOLLAR STRECHER
(subscription every week)

To subscribe to this list, send a message to: *hub@XC.Org*

The subject line is unimportant. In the message body, on the very 1st line write:

subscribe dollar-stretcher

To unsubscribe to this list, you can send mail to:

hub@XC.Org

The subject line is unimportant. In the message body, on the very 1st line write:

unsubscribe dollar-stretcher

If you need further assistance regarding the Dollar-Stretcher contact:

LWilson@xc.org or gary@stretcher.com

HEART & HOME

To subscribe to this list, send a message to:

frugally4u@aol.com

In the subject line write:

subscribe

To unsubscribe to this list, you can send mail to:

frugally4u@aol.com

In the subject line write:

unsubscribe

Internet Links For The Frugal Mom

One Income Living In A Two Income World
http://members.aol.com/DSimple/index.html

The Economic Homemaker
http://www.thecho.com

Tight-Wadding With Doris O'Connell
http://pages.prodigy.com/frugal_tightwad/index.htm

FRUGAL LIVING ONLINE
http://shell.kingston.net/~goju/flo/

FRUGAL LIVING RESOURCES
http://www.econet.org/frugal/

JULIE'S FRUGAL TIPS
http://www.brightok.net/~neilmayo/

FRUGAL CORNER
http://www.frugalcorner.com

THE UNOFFICIAL TIGHTWAD GAZETTE FAN CLUB HOME PAGE
http://users.aol.com/maryfou/tightwad.html

FRUGAL TIPS USA
http://www.geocities.com/Heartland/Flats/2132/money.html

THE DOLLAR STRETCHER
http://www.stretcher.com

FRUGAL BY CHOICE
http://members.aol.com/frugally4u/

FRUGAL LIVING
http://frugalliving.miningco.com/

ONCE-A-MONTH COOKING (OAMC)
http://members.aol.com/OAMCLoop/index.html

ASK MISS FRUGAL
http://member.aol.com/missfrugal/index.html

STAY-AT-HOME MOMS NEWSLETTERS DIRECTORY

MOM SENSE NEWSLETTER
c/o MOPS International
P.O. Box 101750
Denver, CO 80210-1750
$12.00 (donation)/yr/6 issues
Sample issue: free
E-mail address: mopshop@mops.org
Website address: http://www.mops.org

THE PROVERBS 31 HOMEMAKER
Julie Lawing, Editor
P.O. Box 17155
Charlotte, NC 28227
$15.00/yr/12 issues
Sample issue: $1.00
E-mail address: P31home@aol.com
Website address: http://www.scican.net/~mgraphman/P31.html

HEARTS AT HOME NEWSLETTER
Erin Bline, Editor
900 W. College Normal, IL 61761
$15.00/yr/12 issues
Sample issue: $2.00
E-mail address: hearts@dave-world.net
Website address: http://www.hearts-at-home.org

MANIC MOMS NEWSLETTER
Karen Spiegler, Editor
3748 Homestead Rd.
Ravenna, Ohio 44266
$15.00/yr/6 issues
Sample issue: $2.00
E-mail address: manicmoms@prodigy.net
Website address: http://www.parentsplace.com/readroom/manic-moms/index.html

A MOTHER'S MISSION
Karen Ehman, Editor
303 South Traver Street
Saint Johns, MI 48879
$6.00/yr/4 issues
Sample issue: $1.00
E-mail address: Ehman@juno.com

WELCOME HOME NEWSLETTER
Laura Jones, Editor-In-Chief
8310-A Old Courthouse Road
Vienna, VA 22182
$18.00/yr/12 issues
Sample issue: $2.00
E-mail address: mah@mah.org
Website address: http://www.mah.org/

FEMALE FORUM NEWSLETTER
P.O. Box 31
Elmhurst, IL 60126
$24.00/yr/11 issues (includes chapter membership & newsletter)
Sample issue: $1.00 w/ #10 (long) SASE
E-mail address: FEMALEOFC@FEMALEhome.org
Website address: http://FEMALEhome.org/home.htm

STAY AT HOME PARENTING
1325 36th Steet SW
Wyoming, MI 49509
$20.00/yr/12 issues
Sample issue: $1.00 w/ #10 (long) SASE
E-mail address: rdsmith@iserv.net
Website address: http://www.iserv.net/~rdsmith/index.html

THE MOMS JOURNAL
7046 SE Stella Court
Hillsboro, Oregon 97123
$10.00/yr/6 issues
Sample issue: $1.00 w/ #10 (long) SASE
E-mail address: MomIsHome@aol.com

THE PARENTING PAGES
Cynthia Edmonds, Editor
RD 1 Box 1150
Springvale, Maine 04083
$10.00/yr/6 issues
Sample issue: $3.00
E-mail address: redmonds@concentric.net

Internet Links For The Stay At-Home Mom

PARENTS AT HOME PAGE
http://advicom.net/~jsm/moms/

MOMS ONLINE
http://www.momsonline.com/

THE MOMMY TIMES
http://www.mommytimes.com/

THE STAY-AT-HOME MOM'S PAGE
http://www.execpc.com/~russs/

STAY-AT-HOME PARENTS
http://homeparents.miningco.com/

MOM IN THE HOUSE
http://members.aol.com/momnews/

THE STAY-AT-HOME HOMEPAGE
http://members.aol.com/COBLE71/SAHM.html

STAY AT HOME MOMS UNITED
http://www.techroad.com/sahm

Internet Links For The Work At-Home Mom

WORK AT-HOME MOMS
http://www.wahm.com

HOME BASED WORKING MOMS
http://www.hbwm.com/

MOMS NETWORK EXCHANGE
http://www.momsnetwork.com/

BIZY MOMS
http://www.bizymoms.com/

MAILING LISTS/USER GROUPS ON FRUGAL LIVING AND STAYING AT HOME

A mailing list (or user group) is a list of people who share similar interests and can write to everyone in the group at one time. The size of the mailing lists vary from just a few people, to thousands of people.When anyone who belongs to this list responds to a group message, the e-mail is sent to every other person on the list automatically. You subscribe to a list by e-mailing the "list administrator." Normally, you will receive an e-mail confirming your subscription, details about how to post to the mailing list, and how to unsubscribe if you wish to do so later.

Frugal Mail-Lists:

FRUGAL-ED (subscription daily)

To subscribe to this list, send a message to:

listproc@listproc.wsu.edu

The subject line is unimportant. In the message body, on the very 1st line write:

subscribe frugal-ed your_real_name

"Your real name" is just that (i.e. Jane Doe). Send this message and you will be able to send and receive mail from this list.

To receive the digest version of the list (where all messages come together as one message instead of 50 individual messages from each member), send a message to:

listproc@listproc.wsu.edu

The subject line is unimportant. In the message body, on the very 1st line write:

set frugal-ed mail digest

Send this message and you will receive all mail from this list bundled together as one message.

To unsubscribe to the digest version, do the same thing, but write:

"set frugal-ed mail" (without the quotes).

Stay-At-Home Mom Mail-Lists:

SAHM-DIGEST (subscription daily)

To subscribe to digest version of the list (where all messages come together as one message), send a message to:

majordomo@majordomo.net

The subject line is unimportant. In the message body, on the very 1st line write:

subscribe sahm-digest

Send this message and you will receive all mail from this list bundled together as one message.

To unsubscribe to digest version of the list, you can send mail to:

majordomo@majordomo.net

with the following command in the body of your e-mail message:

unsubscribe sahm-digest

If you need further assistance regarding SAHM-DIGEST, e-mail:

blpb@mindspring.com

JUST4MOM'S (subscription daily)

To subscribe to digest version of the list (where all messages come together as one message), send a message to:

Majordomo@doleh.com

The subject line is unimportant. In the message body, on the very 1st line write:

subscribe just4moms-digest

Send this message and you will receive all mail from this list bundled together as one message.

To unsubscribe to digest version of the list, you can send mail to:

Majordomo@doleh.com

with the following command in the body of your e-mail message:

unsubscribe just4moms-digest

If you need further assistance regarding JUST4MOMS digest, e-mail:

owner-just4moms-digest@doleh.com or *dawn@doleh.com*

End Notes

1. *Shattering The Two-Income Myth,* Andy Dappen, 1997, p. 40
2. *Staying Home—From Full-Time Professional To Full-Time Parent,* (Boston Women's Health Book Collective, 1992), p. xiv
3. *Staying Home—From Full-Time Professional To Full-Time Parent,* (Boston Women's Health Book Collective, 1992), p. 215–216
4. *The Stay At Home Mom,* Donna Otto, 1997, p. 27–28
5. *Home By Choice,* Brenda Hunter, 1991
6. *Shattering The Two-Income Myth,* Andy Dappen, 1997, p. 8
7. *Staying Home—From Full-Time Professional To Full-Time Parent,* (Boston Women's Health Book Collective, 1992), p. 217
8. *Staying Home—From Full-Time Professional To Full-Time Parent,* (Boston Women's Health Book Collective, 1992), p. 222
9. *Staying Home—From Full-Time Professional To Full-Time Parent,* (Boston Women's Health Book Collective, 1992), p. 216
10. *Shattering The Two-Income Myth,* Andy Dappen, 1997, p. 7
11. *To Owe Or Not To Owe,* Special Consumer Survey Report by The Conference Board, published in Moody's Weekly Financial Report, June 14, 1996
12. The Business News, 1997
13. *To Owe Or Not To Owe,* Special Consumer Survey Report by The Conference Board, published in Moody's Weekly Financial Report, June 14, 1996
14. *Overcoming Overspending,* Olivia Millan, 1995, Walker & Co., p. 18–19

Index

A

Airline travel 72
Airline phone numbers 78

B

Bankruptcy 93, 93
Budgeting 83

C

Camping 62
Car Buying 155
    New Car 157
    Used Car 160
    Internet Car Buying 163
Car Insurance 105
Car Maintenance 165
    Cause Of Breakdowns 165
    Gasoline 168
    Car Maintenance Checklist 166
    How To Spot A Good Mechanic 170
    Mechanic Helpline 170
    Tires, Buying New 167
    Tire Safety Kit 168
Childcare, Effects Of 13
COBRA 118
Computers For The Technologically Challenged 173
    Computer Terms, Glossary Of 194
    Internet Computer Hardware Retailers 182
    Online Services 185
    Printer Supplies 178
    Repairing Your Computer 183
    Software, Buying 184
    Shareware And Free Software 185

Consumer Rights 197
  Consumer's Responsibility 198
  How To Complain 199
Cost Of Living 18
Cost Of Working 13
Credit Counseling 91

D

Date ideas 76
Debt 82
  Credit Counseling 91
  Debt, Ways To Reduce 89
  Debt Consolidation 92
  Debt Pay Down Plan 89
  Refinance Your Mortgage 90
  Statistics 82
Debtors Support Group 90
Dental And Orthodontic Work 137
Disability Insurance 125
Doctor Bills 127

E

Electronics And Appliances 139
  Energy Consumption Chart 143
  Used Appliances And Electronics 143

F

Family, 3 Keys To A Healthy 18
FEMALE- (Formerly Employed Mothers) 16
Frugality Runamuck 9
Furniture 147
  Tips For Buying 148
  Furnishing Your Home 147
  Furniture Manufacturers 149

G

Gardening 45
  Container Gardening 46
  Homemade Pesticides 49
  How To Compost 49
  How To Start A Garden 45
  Online Gardening 54
  Recipes For Using Excess Crops 50
  Seed Sources 55

H

Hearts At Home 17
HMOs 119
Home exchange 67
Homeowners Insurance 99
    Earthquake Policy 100
Hospital Bills 129
Household Hotlines 141

I

ISPs 186
Identity theft, avoiding 92
Insurance 99
    Dental Expenses 135
    Disability Insurance 125
    Doctor Bills 127
    Flood Insurance 101
    Homeowners Insurance 99
        Earthquake Policy 100
        Mobile Home Insurance 102
        Renter's Insurance 102
    Hospital Bills 129
    Life Insurance 108
        Cash Value Life Insurance 110
        Term Life Insurance 109
        Life Insurance Chart 114
    Medical Insurance 115
        COBRA 118
        HMOs 119
        Medicare 118
        Sharing Groups 117
    Medications 132
        Free Drugs 135
        Generic Names And Purposes For Cold Medications 134
    Vision 126
Internet Car Buying 163
Internet Computer Hardware Retailers 182
Investing 95

K

Kids 21
    Activities 39
    Allowances And Chores 22
    Clothes 28
    Financial Responsibility 21
    Internet use 189

Lunches 25
Snack Recipes 27
Teenagers 25

L

La Leche League 16
Life Insurance 108
Cash Value Life Insurance 110
Life Insurance Chart 114
Term Life Insurance 109

M

Medical Insurance 115
HMOs 119
Sharing Groups 117
Medicare 118
Medications 132
Free Drugs 135
Generic Names And Purposes For Cold Medications 134
Mobile Home Insurance 102
MOMs Club — (Moms Offering Moms Support) 17
MOPS International- (Mothers Of Preschools) 17
Motels 66
Mothers At Home, Inc. 17
Motorhomes 64

N

National At-Home Mother Support Groups 16
No-Debt Lifestyle 82

O

Online services 185

P

Pets 30
Dry Pet Food Recipe 33
Feeding Small Mammals 35
Fleas 37
Pets Food, Biological Value 35
Pet Hotlines 36
Veterinarian Bills 35
Printer Supplies 178

R

Recipes
  Activities For Kids 39
  Dry Pet Food Recipe 33
  For Using Excess Gardening Crops 50
  Homemade Pesticides 49
  Snack Recipes 27
Refinance Your Mortgage 90
Renter's Insurance 102
Repairing Your Computer 183

S

Saving 94
Seed Sources 55
Software, Buying 184
  Shareware And Free Software 185
Snack Recipes 27
Spousal Support 16

T

Teenagers 25
Term Life Insurance 109
Tire Safety Kit 168
Two Income Families 11

U

Used Appliances And Electronics 143

V

Vacations 59
  Lodgings 77
    Campuses 66
    Home exchanges 67
    YMCA 67
Veterinarian Bills 35
Vision care 126

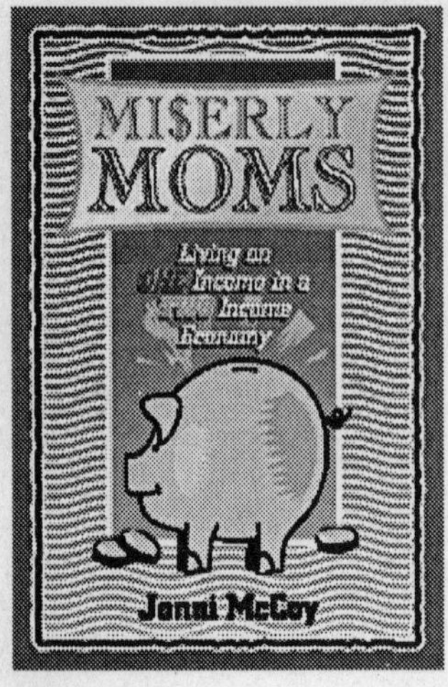

Jonni McCoy is also the author of the bestselling book, *Miserly Moms*. Endorsed by Dr. Laura Schlessinger on her nationally syndicated radio show, the book has found a warm reception among mothers who have decided to leave the work world to stay home full time with their children. Gayle King, daytime television talk show host, has had Jonni on her show twice to help moms see how they can put into practice the hundreds of money-saving hints the book describes.

With nearly 100,000 copies sold, *Miserly Moms* shares with readers how Jonni and her family made the transition from two incomes to one while remaining in the same home in one of the most expensive areas in the entire United States. The "Eleven Miserly Guidelines" will help steer families to success as they trim expenditures on everything from groceries and household cleaners to gas and utilities. With over 250 pages packed with cost-saving techniques, strategies, tips and recipes, *Miserly Moms* has helped families everywhere to live within a one-income budget without feeling "cheap or deprived."

Here's what they're saying about *Miserly Moms*:

"This book offers much-needed encouragement to families who are tired of hearing society's endless whine about the impossibility of mothers staying home to raise their own children. The fact is, it can be done, and it is being done, with ingenuity and good cheer . . . Her 'Eleven Miserly Guidelines' are completely practical, and at the top of the list is the most important: 'Don't confuse frugality with depriving yourself.' "

—*Christian Parenting Today* magazine

"Let Jonni McCoy be your guide through the jungle of 'hidden' costs, misleading purchasing assumptions, and costly habits. She leads you out of the murky water of living up to the unrealistic standards of our society into the calmness of balanced checkbooks and a peaceable home life."

—Jill Bond, author of *Dinner's in the Freezer!*

For more information, check out Jonni's web site:
http://www.miserlymoms.com